GW00760982

UNIFORMS OF THE SS

VOLUME 2
GERMANISCHE-SS 1940-1945

Hugh Page Taylor

Windrow & Greene

Third edition
© 1991 Historical Research Unit
Illustrated by Malcolm McGregor

All rights reserved. No part of this publication may
be reproduced or transmitted in any form or by any means,
electronic or mechanical, including photocopy, recording,
or in any information storage and retrieval system,
without the prior written consent of the publishers.

Published in Great Britain 1991 by
Windrow & Greene Ltd.
5 Gerrard Street
London W1V 7LJ

Printed and bound in Great Britain by
Butler & Tanner Ltd, Frome and London

British Library Cataloguing in Publication Data

Uniforms of the SS. – 3rd ed.
Vol. 2: Germanische-SS 1940–1945
I. Taylor, Hugh Page
355.140943

ISBN 1–872004–95–4

FOREWORD TO THIRD EDITION

Unlike most other branches of the SS, little was known about the Germanic SS before the first edition of this book appeared in 1969. I had opened files by the early 1960s on the Dutch, Flemish, and Norwegian Germanic SS organizations, as well as the Danish Schalburg Corps and Germanic Battalions; but real progress only came in 1965, a year which I had the pleasure of spending in Oslo. Even so, co-operation from archives and libraries varied considerably from one country to another. It was perhaps no coincidence that the most difficult subject to study was the Schalburg Corps, the 'odd man out' amongst the four branches of the Germanic SS, which some still maintain should not be defined as a branch of the Germanic SS at all. Very little material was forthcoming from Denmark before the publication of the first edition; and I had to rely mainly upon contemporary Allied Intelligence reports, and information supplied by military historians.

The quantity and quality of available information and illustrations also varied. The Germanic SS in Flanders, Holland and Norway all had their own newspapers, which provided some valuable facts and photographs, despite limitations imposed by wartime security. No such specific source existed for the Danish Schalburg Corps; but I was fortunate enough to receive help from the late Col. C. M. Dodkins, who also gave permission for the use of some of his exclusive photographs. The situation changed drastically after publication of the first edition. Individuals and institutions alike provided a mass of new material, answering old questions, filling in gaps, and raising new problems. Sources which had previously cast doubt on the very existence of a Germanic SS organization in their country suddenly "discovered" that they did in fact have information, including documents, badges, and even complete uniforms. Our knowledge of the subject thus grew dramatically in the year following publication of the first edition; and I was delighted when Andrew Mollo agreed to a completely revised second edition which appeared in 1970.

Fresh material found over the intervening 20 years has been negligible in comparison; and so this third edition goes to press unchanged other than for this new foreword. Research into archives in Germany and the four countries concerned has revealed next to nothing. Scrutiny of the personnel records of SS officers held in the much-abused Berlin Document Centre has unearthed little of relevance, mainly because few files relating to non-Germans are held there. Correspondence with former members of the Germanic SS has also been disappointing, and has naturally declined with the passage of time. A retired German SS-Standartenführer who had played a key role in the recruitment of Germanics for the Waffen-SS was found in Munich, and interviewed; but his memory of and interest in those far-off events had faded, replaced by a far keener interest in religion.

Even in the second edition there were badges which we had to illustrate with artist's impressions, as originals were not available. One of these (the extremely rare civilian lapel pin of the Norges SS/Germanske SS Norge) has since been located, and it is gratifying that our artist's impression proved so accurate that no change is required. The badge had "GSSN", with the "SS" in runes, etched on the reverse.

It is to be hoped that researchers will one day come across full details of the Germanic Battalions, perhaps the least-known branch of the SS organization. An interesting top secret memorandum dated 3 March 1944, from the Waffen-SS recruiting chief SS-Obergruppenführer Gottlob Berger to Dr. Brandt of Himmler's personal staff, contains the comment: "The Germanic SS battalions have a current strength of 2,179. The reason why they are so small is that they are always being creamed off for Sennheim."

The Germanic SS has been covered in books and magazine articles which have appeared over the past two decades. The authors have paid us the compliment of copying our work, but their lack of fresh material and failure to use primary sources have led to nothing of value or interest that justifies inclusion in this third edition. Yet I am the first to admit that there is still much more to learn; and I would be more than grateful for any information that readers of this edition can supply: answering questions raised, filling in gaps (especially in the orders-of-battle and lists of officers and their commands), or bringing to light as yet unrecorded details. Who knows: a revised fourth edition may one day be possible.

My sincere thanks and gratitude to all those who have helped with my research over the years must again be recorded, particularly to the following institutions and individuals:

Det kongelige Bibliotek, Copenhagen
Museet for Danmarks Frihedskamp 1940–45, Copenhagen
Tøjhusmuseet, Copenhagen
New York Public Library, New York
Norsk Telegrambyraa A/S, Oslo
Universitetsbiblioteket, Oslo
Rijksinstituut voor Oorlogsdocumentatie, Amsterdam
Stadsarchief, Antwerp

Markus Anaja; Egon Alois Bartetzko; Alan Beadle; Philip H. Buss; Mrs. Ingeborg Christmas-Møller; Albert Denis; Col. C. M. Dodkins CBE,

DSO; Albert Eyns; Hartvig Fleege; J. Govaerts; Sven-Erik Halvorsen; Eric Kjellberg; David Littlejohn; Dr. André Mathias; Andrew Mollo; Inga Fl. Rasmussen; Sverre Scott; P. van Dijke; Drs. N. K. C. A. in't Veld; Count Ernesto Vitetti.

Hugh Page Taylor
Milan, Italy
February 1991

INTRODUCTION

This is the second book in a series devoted to the uniforms and insignia of the SS, and yet already marks a drastic change in content and approach to the first (''Volume 1: Allgemeine-SS'' by Andrew Mollo). For whereas the major part of Volume 1 was taken up with illustrations and photographs, with only short historical and organizational surveys, the very subject-matter of Volume 2—the Germanic SS—makes such a format impossible. The reason for this is simply that in contrast to the Allgemeine-SS in Germany, the Germanic SS was small and comparatively short-lived, and consequently its uniforms and insignia were limited in complexity and variation. Much more attention has therefore been paid to details of historical background and development, and the organization of each branch has been presented in as much detail and depth as the severely limited sources (both primary and otherwise) allow. This in no way suggests a limitation to uniform and insignia coverage, however, which is the real purpose of this series, and all relevant details and illustrations available have been included.

Another difference between this book and Volume 1 is that whereas much has been written about the SS and its German political section the Allgemeine-SS, virtually nothing has appeared in the English language on the Germanic SS; and whereas foreign references are available on the four individual branches, nothing to my knowledge has ever been written on the subject as a whole. So before starting this book a definition of the Germanic SS will probably be in order for most of its readers.

The Germanic SS (''Germanische SS'') is the term used exclusively to describe the political non-German SS formations in the Germanic countries. In turn, ''Germanic'' (''Germanen'') was used by Himmler and the SS to denote non-Germans of so-called ''Nordic blood'', who were to be found mainly in Holland, the Flemish areas of Belgium, Norway, Denmark, Sweden, and areas of Switzerland, the United States and Great Britain. Himmler was anxious to have ''Germanics'' from such countries in the SS, and as early as 1938 had authorized their acceptance into the SS-Verfügungstruppe. But before the war

very few were available and willing to join the SS—by the end of 1938 there were but 20 such volunteers, and the Übersichtsplan of May 4th, 1940, lists only 100, including 5 from the United States, 3 from Sweden and 44 from Switzerland. It was the coming of the Second World War and the subsequent imposition of the German fear of Communism that urged Dutchmen, Belgians, Norwegians and Danes to enlist in the SS in two distinct ways.

Firstly, and during the early stages of their respective occupations by the Germans, they went into the Waffen-SS, with Norwegians and Danes joining SS-Standarte (Regiment) ''Nordland'', and Dutchmen and Flemings going to SS-Standarte ''Westland'' (''Nordland'' and ''Westland'' were ordered by Hitler on April 20th, 1940, and May 25th, 1940, respectively). Most of these Germanic volunteers joined for no better reason than to seek adventure, and the National Socialists amongst them were in the minority. Once war was declared on Russia, however, these volunteers could justify their membership of the SS on the grounds that they were combat troops fighting Bolshevism in the defence of their homelands. But the second phase of Germanic enrolment into the SS, that of the Germanic SS itself and the subject of this book, was far harder to justify, for rather than combat troops they were part of a political extension of the German Allgemeine-SS in their respective countries.

All four branches of the Germanic SS—Dutch, Flemish, Norwegian and Danish—were in countries already having National Socialist parties before the war. Each of these Nazi parties collaborated with the Germans, and served them on the understanding that in so doing they would preserve, in a post-war Germanic Europe, their own national independence. They were forced, therefore, to pay lip-service to the Germanic idea, but really sought a loosely-knit Germanic Confederation, in which their countries would be independent and self-governing National Socialist states.

Himmler may have been sincere when he preached Germanic ideology, and with it the unity and equality of Germanic blood, but certain of the highest SS leaders did not see matters quite in that way. They looked on the Germanic countries as mere districts (''Gaue'') of Germany, which would not be allowed individually to control their own affairs. Consequently the aim of the Germanic SS in their respective countries was diametrically opposed to that of the national Nazi parties. In all but Denmark one will find repeated opposition between the two. Mussert in Holland was cool towards the SS from the time of its arrival, and grew more hostile as the war progressed. Staf de Clercq's V.N.V. opposed the Flemish SS bitterly, and Quisling in Norway even went

iii

so far as to oppose the Norwegian SS in public, and was all but insulting to Himmler. In view of this opposition, Himmler, Berger the head of the SS-Hauptamt, the "Higher SS and Police Leaders" in each country and their subordinates, did their best to undermine the local Nazi parties and remove them from the political scene. Such attempts aggravated the situation, but did not in fact meet with complete success.

The status of the Germanic SS varied from one country to another. In Denmark and Flanders it was independent of the local Nazi leader and party, in Norway and Holland it was a formation of the local party and therefore theoretically subordinate to the local Nazi leader. Effectively, however, the leadership over all branches of the Germanic SS was exercised by Himmler's personal representative in each country. In particular they were subordinate to the respective Germanische Leitstelle, which was in turn responsible to both the HSSuPf, and the head office of the Germanische Leitstelle in Berlin—a sub-division of Berger's SS-Hauptamt.

The Germanic SS was directed from the SS Main Office (SS-Hauptamt) in Berlin, headed by SS-Obergruppenführer und General der Waffen-SS Gottlob Berger. Within this Main Office it formed Department D II (Amt D II) which was led by SS-Obersturmbannführer Max Kopischke (formerly on the staff of SS-Junkerschule "Bad Tölz"). Department D II was further divided into two Sections (Abteilungen) as follows:

Section D II 1a (Abteilung D II 1a): The Germanic SS in Germany (Germanische-SS im Reich), led by SS-Untersturmführer Johannes Gustke. Contained a Section Head (Referent) for each of the following: Flanders, Holland, Switzerland and Denmark.*

Section D II 1b (Abteilung D II 1b): The Germanic SS abroad (Germanische-SS in den Ländern). Contained a Section Head (Referent) for each of the following: Flanders, Holland and Switzerland/Denmark.*

Also controlled by Department D (Amtsgruppe D) of the SS Main Office was the "Germanic SS 'House Germanien' Hildesheim Political Leadership School" (Germanische Schutzstaffel Haus Germanien Hildesheim Politische Führerschule), commanded by SS-Sturmbannführer (F) Dr. Peter Paulsen.

The basic character of the four branches of the Germanic SS was similar, but on close inspection differed in many respects. For a start, all included the name of their country in their title, except for the Danish

* No reason has been found for the exclusion of Norway from this list.

branch, which by calling itself the "Schalburg-Korps" was the only exponent of the "personality cult". The uniform which was based on that of the German SS bore different insignia, having only the system of rank badges and the death's head on the cap common to all. The Germanic SS sleeve badge (silver SS runes on a black diamond) was worn on different sides by the Dutch, Flemish and Norwegians, but not by the Danes. The Scandinavian Danish and Norwegian SS wore their respective versions of the circular swastika, while the Lowland Dutch and the Flemish followed the German SS practice of wearing regimental numbers. The Dutch and Norwegians also wore SS versions of their respective party emblems, while the Danish wore a national, as opposed to a political emblem. The Flemish wore no national arm badge at all.

Switzerland, in spite of being a neutral country throughout World War II, was considered suitable for a Germanic SS formation. Swiss affairs were managed by Branch DI/3 (Amtsgruppe DI/3) of the SS Main Office under H. Bueler and Paul Benz, and this branch established "Panorama-Heim" in Stuttgart to attract Swiss nationals living in Germany and to induce them to join the SS. In 1944 Franz Riedweg received orders to establish a Swiss SS organization, under the name "Schweizer Sportbund" (Swiss Sports League), but all the same retaining the all-important initials. Later, Paul Benz wrote a memorandum to Himmler in which he suggested the establishment of not only a Swiss Waffen-SS unit, a Germanische Leitstelle Schweiz, and an Ersatzkommando Schweiz der Waffen-SS, but also a Swiss branch of the Germanic SS ("Germanische-SS Schweiz"). This memorandum was brought to Himmler's attention on November 27th, 1944, and by December the 1st Section Heads were in existence for the Swiss in both Section DII 1a and DII 1b of the SS Main Office (for Swiss Germanic SS in Germany and Switzerland respectively). The war was soon over, however, and no record has so far come to light to suggest that the Swiss Germanic SS ever got beyond the planning stage.

In conclusion it must be emphasized that the Germanic SS represented only a very small section of the SS complex as a whole, and was made up of a minute number of collaborators from each of the four countries concerned. The impressive-sounding tables of units to be found under all sections should under no circumstances be taken at face value, for they were severely undermanned and some may not have existed at all, being mere entries on paper.

The Germanic SS movement was negligible in size and viewed with distaste by the vast majority of the people of Holland, Belgium, Norway and Denmark.

CONTENTS

Page

TITLES OF UNITS OF THE GERMANIC SS, DATES OF FORMATION AND RENAMING

	COUNTRY	FORMATION	ORIGINAL TITLE(S)	RENAMED	FINAL TITLE
1	Holland	11.9.1940	Algemeene SS in Nederland/ Nederlandsche SS	1.11.1942	Germaansche SS (in) Nederland
2	Belgium	—.9.1940	Algemeene SchutScharen Vlaanderen/ Algemeene SS Vlaanderen/ Algemeene Vlaamsche SS/ Vlaamsche SS/ SS-Vlaanderen	1.10.1942	Germaansche SS (in) Vlaanderen
2a	Belgium	1.9.1941(?)	SS-Militie	1.8.1942	Vlaanderen-Korps
3	Norway	21.5.1941	Norges SS	21.7.1942	Germanske SS Norge
4	Denmark	2.2.1943	(Germansk Korps)	?	Schalburgkorps
5	Switzerland	—	Germanische SS Schweiz[1]	—	—

1. Planned but not formed.

HISTORY OF THE DUTCH SS

Motto: a) Mijn Eer Mijn Trouw

b) Mijn Eer Heet Trouw

Apart from Germany, the Netherlands had possibly more National Socialists before the war than any other European country, and they were found in many different Nazi parties. There were no less than seven copies of the German N.S.D.A.P., all named the Netherlands National Socialist Workers Party ("Nationaal-Socialistische Nederlandsche Arbeiders Partij" or "N.S.N.A.P."). Most of these were very small with scarcely more members than the leader and his staff. The most important among them, but still on a small scale, were those led by Major C. J. A. Kruyt, which petered out in the summer of 1940, and its rival led by Dr. E. H. Ridder van Rappard. Both of these parties worked for the absorption of Holland in a Greater Germany, but under occupation the Germans soon realized that neither could ever attract sufficient support to be worth while. They therefore turned their attention to another party, the National Socialist Movement ("Nationaal-Socialistische Beweging" or "N.S.B."), led by Dipl. Ing. Anton Adriaan Mussert. Mussert strongly disliked and objected to van Rappard's N.S.N.A.P. and brought about its disbandment during a visit to Hitler in Berlin on December 12th, 1941. Exactly what was said is not known, but the N.S.N.A.P. was ordered by the German authorities to disband just two days later, and during the next few months its members were absorbed into the N.S.B. The other Nazi parties were still in existence by then but had lost what small influence they had ever had, and were dissolved at the same time.

The N.S.B. was formed in December 1931 by Mussert and was consequently one of the first Nazi-style parties created outside Germany. It achieved a certain amount of success during the mid-thirties when considerable discontent prevailed in Holland. In the provincial elections of 1935 it reached its pre-war peak with 7.94% of the total votes and two seats in the Upper House. Two years later at the general election of 1937 its poll had dropped to 4.22% with four seats in both Upper and Lower Houses, and in the provincial elections of 1939 it was down further to 3.89% with three seats in the Upper and four in the Lower House. This progressive decline in Dutch National Socialism before World War Two was produced by various factors, including political developments abroad (especially in Germany), the rising standard of living and the fall of unemployment in Holland, and the sharp opposition from almost all sections of the Dutch community. Under occupation actual membership naturally increased, and whereas only 28,000 members are listed in May 1940, about 100,000 are reported by the end of 1942.

In November 1932 Mussert followed Hitler's earlier example and formed a group of stormtroopers to defend him in brawls and agitate and fight with the Communists, and this was named the Weerafdeeling, or W.A., paralleling the S.A. in Germany. Mussert disbanded it in 1935 but in 1939 created the "Mussert-Garde", by name a bodyguard to Mussert, but in effect a revival of the W.A. The "Mussert-Garde" was formed by J. Hendrik ("Henk") Feldmeijer who had been born in 1910, joined the N.S.B. in 1932 as Party Member 479 and in so doing forfeited his rank of Lieutenant in the Dutch Army. The Mussert Guard was without doubt intended by Feldmeijer as a sort of SS, and it can be considered as the organizational forerunner of the Dutch SS. In effect Feldmeijer later converted it into the Dutch SS, which he was also destined to lead.

Variations of commemorative badges of former members of the "Mussert-Garde"; central discs red.

Germany invaded the Netherlands on May 10th, 1940, and the Dutch Army was forced to surrender on the 14th. On May 19th Dr. Arthur Seyss-Inquart was named Reichskommissar (Plenipotentiary) for the Netherlands and he took up his office on the 29th. He ruled and administered occupied Holland through four German commissar generals (Generalkommissare), two of whom (Wimmer and Fischböck) held honorary SS rank, and one, Hanns Albin Rauter, had been appointed by Himmler on May 23rd "Höherer SS- und Polizeiführer und Generalkommissar für das Sicherheitswesen" (Higher SS and Police Leader and Commissar General for Security Matters) in Holland. Rauter arrrived on May 25th holding the rank of an SS-Brigadeführer und Generalmajor der Polizei, but he was later promoted and finally held the rank of SS-Obergruppenführer und General der Waffen-SS und Polizei. From almost the beginning of the occupation Rauter assumed command of the Dutch police.

During the first year of the German occupation the Dutch were allowed limited political freedom, but long before the official dissolution of the democratic political parties in June, 1941, their activities were hampered, if not rendered impossible. Thus at first there was a token of democratic politics in Holland and it was not until the end of 1942 that the highly unpopular Dutch Nazis under Mussert were granted any measure of authority, and even then this was very slight. Mussert had his "Mussert Guard" but from the beginning of the occupation had been cool towards the SS and was therefore unwilling to have a political SS formed in the Netherlands. But the Allgemeine-SS in Germany were determined to establish a branch in the Netherlands and the possibility of forming a "Dutch General SS" ("Algemeene SS in Nederland") was put to Mussert by Seyss-Inquart in late August 1940. He was forced to agree and in fact it was Mussert himself, in his capacity of "Leider" (leader) of the N.S.B., that established this Dutch political SS formation. It was named the "Nederlandsche SS" ("Dutch SS"), was officially established on September 11th, 1940, as "a formation ("formatie") of the N.S.B." and organized within the headquarters of the N.S.B. first as Department IX of the Staff H.Q. ("Afdeeling IX van het Hoofdkwartier") and after the reorganization of the N.S.B. in 1942 as Main Department IX of the N.S.B. ("Hoofdafdeeling IX van de N.S.B.") There was almost certainly no official foundation ceremony, for Feldmeijer had collected his men together piece-meal. The original 150 men came partly from the Mussert Guard, while others were old W.A. members. In late 1940 and early 1941 they were joined by some volunteers from the SS-Standarte "Westland" as they returned home from Germany, and in fact one of the original intentions of Himmler and Berger, when they set up "Westland" in 1940, was to provide a core for a forthcoming Dutch political SS. These men were particularly welcome to the Dutch SS as they brought with them experience in German SS training and methods. The advisor to the Dutch SS was SS-Standartenführer R. Jungclaus (later appointed HSSuPf in Belgium—see under the Flemish SS section), who was a member of Rauter's staff at the time. Prospective members had to be able to prove Aryan descent back to 1800 (for officers it was 1750), be not less than 1.72 meters in height, and be between 18 and 35 years of age. They had to pay a contribution of 1 florin per month and pay for their own uniform. On September 16th, 1940, Feldmeijer was appointed Voorman, or commander, of the Dutch SS and in an article in the 27th of September issue of the N.S.B.'s newspaper "Volk en Vaderland" he introduced his new formation to the Dutch people.

The existence of both the Dutch SS and the W.A. was authorized by Seyss-Inquart on November 1st, 1940, and both were left nominally as formations of the N.S.B. and under Mussert's command. Like the W.A., the Dutch SS was therefore a para-military formation of

the N.S.B. but in practice it paid obedience only to Himmler and was but a tool of his representative in Holland—Rauter. It held its first parade in the Hague on January 11th, 1941, and on February 22nd, 1941, a large rally was held for them in the City-Theater in Amsterdam and there followed a massed march-past through the streets of the capital.

In March 1941 the Dutch SS was reported as having some 600 members. On May 17th, 1942, Mussert handed the Dutch SS over to Himmler at a ceremony held in Amsterdam—it was a move described at the time as "the incorporation of the Dutch SS into the Germanic SS", and it was "received into the SS Order and Community with all rights, duties and laws that this involved." Himmler also honoured them with the right to wear the German SS belt buckle with the motto "Meine Ehre heisst Treue" (Ref: Der Reichsführer-SS, Führerhauptquartier, den 23. Juni 1942, Tgb.Nr. RF/V.) This point marked the formal transfer of allegiance of the Dutch SS to Hitler, Himmler and the German SS proper, (although it still continued to be a formation of the N.S.B.) and at this ceremony the only concession given to Mussert was that he took the oath of allegiance from the Dutch SS personally. This oath was given to Hitler and ran as follows:

> "Adolf Hitler, leader of the Germanic peoples, I swear loyal and faithful obedience unto you, and those that you place in authority over me, unto death. So truly help me God!"
> ("Adolf Hitler, Germaansche Führer, U zweer ik hou en trouw en U en de door U over mij gestelden gehoorzaamheid tot in de dood. Zo waarlijk helpe mij God!")

At this ceremony the full complement of the Germanic SS in Holland is reported as 750 men.

The actual status of the Dutch SS was, to say the least, confusing, and it remained ambiguous to the end. It owed its allegiance to the N.S.B. and the SS rather than to Holland or Germany. It was said to have been

The commander of the Dutch SS (Voorman der Nederlandsche SS) J. H. Feldmeijer.

above state level, a pan-Germanic organization, working for the Greater Germanic State (het groot-Germaansche Rijk) so in this way it strived for quite a different goal to that of Mussert and his N.S.B., for whereas the latter worked and fought for a greater Holland (and with it union with Flanders and the creation of a great Union of the Netherlands), the Dutch SS was consciously working for a Germanic Reich. In turn this aim differed from the real objective of the SS as a whole, which was to create a German Reich with a country such as Holland as a mere district ("Gau"). This policy was supported by a number of the highest German SS leaders, although Himmler was careful in public to keep to the Germanic concept.

The result of the conflict in objectives between SS and N.S.B. was considerable friction, and one can appreciate Mussert's distrust (if not dislike) of the Dutch SS. Holland was consequently the first Germanic country in which the indigenous Nazi leader and the indigenous political SS did not see eye to eye, and it was not to be the last.

The Nederlandsche SS was renamed on November 1st, 1942, "Germanic SS in the Netherlands" ("Germaansche SS in Nederland"), to bring their title in line with the other existing Germanic SS formations. This renaming also made quite clear to those that had not already realized it, that the real control of the Dutch SS was not exercised by Mussert and his Dutch Nazi Movement, but by Himmler and his SS empire. The truth is that Mussert had never held any control over the formation at all.

Feldmeijer held his post of "Voorman" of the Dutch SS from the date of his appointment on September 16th, 1940, until his death in an air raid on February 22nd, 1945. His term of office was, however, interrupted by his active service in the Waffen-SS and while he was away he handed his command temporarily over to other officers. Feldmeijer served with the Leibstandarte SS "Adolf Hitler" in the Balkan campaign of the spring of 1941, and later with the "Wiking" Division in Russia, where he was wounded at Kalmuk. His rank of Voorman was a special and unique one, but in March 1943 it was decided to grant him a regular SS rank and he

was appointed a Standartenführer in the Germanic SS. At the same time he was an Untersturmführer der Waffen-SS, being promoted to Hauptsturmführer der Waffen-SS at the end of 1944. But although the Voorman was the most senior rank in the Dutch SS, it was in turn subordinate to the HSSuPf in Holland, Rauter. Furthermore, in mid-1941 Mussert appointed C. Van Geelkerken as supervisor of all the para-military formations of the N.S.B., and as this included W.A., Jeugdstorm (the Dutch Nazi youth organization) and Dutch SS he theoretically became Feldmeijer's superior. Effectively, Feldmeijer was always subordinate to Himmler, and Himmler's representative in Holland, Rauter.

In March 1943 Feldmeijer said "every man in the Dutch SS, so far as he is physically capable, must see service at the front . . . in principle every SS man should report for service at the front, although we cannot let everybody go since we must further build up the Germanic SS in Holland". He was strongly in favour of his political SS men following his own example and serving with the Waffen-SS at the front, and he actually introduced conscription for this purpose, notably for the SS Freiwilligen-Grenadier-Brigade "Landstorm Nederland", and in late 1944 tried to bring unwilling members to court-martial.

At the beginning of September 1944 Field Marshal Bernard Montgomery's army entered North Brabant and on September 5th the Germans and Dutch Nazis began to leave. On April 30th, 1945 Seyss-Inquart proclaimed to all the Germans left in "Fortress Holland" the news of Hitler's death, and on May 5th, 1945 the German 25th Army under General Johannes von Blaskowitz surrendered to the Canadian general Charles Foulkes. With the liberation the first of the Germanic SS organizations to have been formed in an occupied country was extinguished. The last register of members of the Dutch SS contained 6,127 names*.

*This figure includes Dutchmen living in Germany, and consequently may well have included the Germanische Sturmbanne (see Page 70). The highest membership number in the Dutch SS itself so far found is 3,727, but this may be well under the actual total.

SCHOLING
Training

Originally there was no centralized training for the Dutch SS. Dutch volunteers for SS-Standarte "Westland" of the Waffen-SS went to Munich for training, and as a number of these eventually joined the Dutch SS, Munich can be considered as the initial training for that organization. But it was not until May 1st, 1941, that a school for the Dutch SS was opened, and this was SS-school Avegoor, situated in a large white mansion in extensive grounds at Ellecom, near Arnheim. It was intended as a para-military and indoctrination centre for the Dutch SS as well as other members of the N.S.B., policemen, sports instructors and so on. The courses varied from one to six weeks, and for the Dutch SS covered racial and ideological fields, with lectures on such subjects as the SS in general, the N.S.D.A.P., the Dutch SS itself, the security police, the civil police, 'blood and soil', the Germanic heroes of the past, German history and so on. Semi-military training was carried out and military sport formed an important part of the school's programme (to such an extent that an Allied intelligence report of June 1943 even described Avegoor as a physical training camp for the Germanic SS).

In March 1943 the name of the school was altered to SS-Ausbildungs-lager Avegoor, although no other changes were made. These came in September 1944 when the Germans were obliged through the adverse results of the war to move the school to Hoogeveen (province of Drenthe), where it was completely militarized and became, with fresh volunteers from the N.S.B. and elsewhere, the Field Replacement Battalion (Feld-Ersatz-Bataillon) of the SS Volunteer Grenadier Brigade "Landstorm Nederland" (SS-Freiwilligen-Grenadier-Brigade "Landstorm Neder-land"). It was basically for this unit that Feldmeijer had introduced conscription in the Dutch SS, and the Replacement Battalion formed from the old Dutch SS School actually provided a large number of recruits during the winter of 1944/1945. Although "Landstorm Nederland" never exceeded Brigade strength it was eventually upgraded to a nominal division, and numbered the 34th.

The school was commanded from the very beginning by a German SS-Hauptsturmführer, Dr. Alois (Alfons?) J. Brendel, who was later promoted to SS-Sturmbannführer and took command of the Replacement Battalion. His permanent German staff were considered as full members of the Waffen-SS, and included SS-Obersturmführer Horst Schwertfeger, SS-Untersturmführer Hauck, and a small number of NCOs. Brendel was absent from May to September, 1942, serving with the 5th SS Armoured Division "Wiking", during which time Schwertfeger took over temporary command of the school. The Dutch SS school was under the control of the SS-Hauptamt, and in particular the Germanische Leitstelle.

ORGANISATIE
Organization

The Staff and District organization of the Nederlandsche SS/Germaansche SS in Nederland is given below and the former is differentiated from the latter where necessary.

As with the N.S.B. itself, the Staff Headquarters of the Dutch SS were originally in Utrecht, first at Catharijnesingel 117, then in April 1941 at Maliebaan 66. There they remained (with the exception of a report of being at Rijksstraatweg 1 in April 1943) until September 1944, when all N.S.B. and SS organization in Holland was thrown into utter confusion by the Allied successes in the West. The Dutch SS Staff H.Q. moved first to Emmalaan 34 in Apeldoorn, then in November 1944 to Westersingel 19, and Kraneweg 19, Groningen. No clear picture has emerged from the chaotic days of September 1944 covering the panic-stricken moves of all the SS bureaux, and both Feldmeijer and his Staff H.Q. certainly set themselves up at addresses that have not so far come to light.

The departments of the Staff H.Q. of the Dutch SS are given in the following table:

NEDERLANDSCHE SS

GERMAANSCHE SS IN NEDERLAND

VOORMAN : J. H. Feldmeijer
Commander
STAFCHEF : SS-Opperstormleider J. L. Jansonius
Chief-of-Staff

STAFLEIDING DER NEDERLANDSCHE SS
Staff Leadership of the Ned.-SS

STAFLEIDING DER GERMAANSCHE SS
IN NEDERLAND
Staff Leadership of the Germ. SS in Holland

Afd. IA : ORGANISATIE EN SCHOLING
    Organization & training
Afd. IB : PERS EN PROPAGANDA
    Press & propaganda

Afd. I   A : SCHOLING
    Training

Afd. I   O : ORGANISATIE
    Organization
Afd. I   Fürs. : SOLDAAT EN SIBBE
    Welfare : Soldier & genealogy
Afd. I   Sp : SPORTLEIDING
    Sport leadership

Afd. II : PERSONEEL
    Personnel
Afd. III : RECHTSPRAAK
    Legal section
Afd. IV : BEHEER EN BEGUNSTIGENDE LEDEN
    Administration & aiding members

Afd. V : MEDISCHE ZAKEN
    Medical section
Afd. VI : OPNEMING EN WERVING
    Admission & recruitment
Afd. VII :   —

Afd. II PERSONEEL
    Personnel
Afd. III RECHTSZAKEN
    Legal section
Afd. IV BEHEER
    Administration
    BEG. LEDEN
    Aiding members
Afd. V MED. DIENST
    Medical service
Afd. VI OPNAME
    Acceptance of aspirants
Afd. VII A : VORMING (SS-VORMINGSAMBT)
    Education
    RADIO
    Radio

NEDERLANDSCHE-SS

GERMAANSCHE SS IN NEDERLAND

Afd. PERS

Press

Afd. PROP.

Propaganda

Afd. VIII A : VORMING

Education

B : SS-RAS- EN SIBBEAMBT

SS Race & genealogy department

C : SOLDAAT EN SIBBE

Soldier & genealogy

FOTO- EN FILMDIENST

Photographic & film service

TAMBOER- EN PIJPERKORPS

Drum & fife corps

HOOFDREDACTEUR "STORM"

Chief editor of "Storm"

HOOFDREDACTEUR "HAMER"

Chief editor of "Hamer"

GERMAANSCHE WERKGEMEENSCHAP
NEDERLAND
Germanic Research Association Holland.

Ref. "N.S. Jaarboek 1942"

Ref. "N.S. Almanak 1944"

DISTRICT ORGANIZATION

By the end of 1943 the Dutch SS was organized into five local regiments ("Standaarden") and one SS Police regiment ("Politie-Standaard"). These regiments, together with the addresses of their regimental H.Q.s and their districts are listed below. In theory each "Standaard" contained 1,550 men (excluding staff), divided into 3 Storm-bannen. Each Stormban should have consisted of 500 men (again excluding staff), divided into 4 Stormen. Each Storm of 175 men was divided into 3 Troepen, of 41 men each, which were divided into 4 Groepen of 10 men each. It should be remembered, however, that the manpower of the Dutch SS was constantly being tapped for combat duty in the Waffen-SS and so all units were severely under strength and some may even have ceased to exist at times.

SS REGIMENT		NAME	REGT. H.Q.	DISTRICT
1. SS-Standaard	—	Groningen	Kraneweg 19	Friesland, Groningen & Drenthe
2. SS-Standaard	—	Arnheim (Arnhem)	Sw. de Landasstraat	Overijssel & Gelderland
3. SS-Standaard	—	Amsterdam	Koningslaan 12	North Holland & Utrecht
4. SS-Standaard	—	The Hague (Den Haag)	Groenhovenstraat 12	South Holland & Zeeland
5. SS-Standaard	—	Eindhoven	Ten Hagestraat 1	North Brabant & Limburg

SS-Politie-Standaard: Directorate-General of the Police, Section: S III, Post Box 71, Nijmegen.

The SS Police Regiment (SS-Politie-Standaard) was commanded by SS-Onderstormleider L. Broersen, who was at the same time Plenipotentiary for the reorganization of the Dutch police, and therefore virtual chief of the Dutch police under Rauter. It consisted of members of the police, who appear to have continued to wear their Dutch police uniforms.

In addition to the above numbered regiments and the police regiment, the Dutch SS was represented in each district of the N.S.B. by a Commandant ("Commandant Germaansche SS in Nederland"—Ref. Organization Chart of an N.S.B. District, N.S.B. H.Q., Utrecht, November 1942).

Ref. "N.S. Almanak 1944".

BEGUNSTIGENDE LEDEN
Aiding members

Financially the Dutch SS was backed from the funds given to the N.S.B. by the Reichskommissar, and from the millions the "Reichsschatzmeister der N.S.D.A.P." gave to the SS for its political work outside Germany. But following the example of the German SS "Aiding Members" (Fördernde Mitglieder" or "F.M."), Feldmeijer established a parallel Dutch SS organization in 1941. This was called the "Instituut der Begunstigende Leden der Germaansche SS in Nederland", referred to normally as "Begunstigende Leden" or "B.L.", meaning "favouring (or aiding) members". The Dutch were therefore offered the opportunity of donating to the funds of the Dutch SS without actually becoming full members, and for this they were issued with a special lapel badge to be worn on civilian dress.

Contributions could be as large as one pleased, but there was a minimum of one florin per month and twelve florins per year. But whereas the aiding members of the SS in Germany were mere contributors, Feldmeijer planned a much more important role for the B.L. in Holland, for he wished them to become a political SS reserve force. To this end in 1942 he forced the B.L. to sign a pledge, containing the oath of allegiance to Hitler that the active members of the Dutch SS had taken on May 17th. But ultimately he never achieved his aim, and the B.L. never constituted anything other than mere contributors.

In May 1942 only 850 B.L. are reported, but by 1944 the number had risen to four thousand.

Lapel badge for Aiding Members (B.L.) of the Dutch SS.

THE BLACK SS SERVICE UNIFORM

Unlike the Flemish and the Norwegian branches of the Germanic SS, the Dutch SS did not have a first pattern uniform, but were issued with the black service uniform at the beginning. The HSSuPf in Holland, Rauter, had already stockpiled uniforms in July 1940 which are believed to have been of German manufacture. Subsequent uniforms issued to the Dutch SS are thought to have been made in Holland, and they also used made-over W.A. uniforms. Although they followed the German design these uniforms reflected Dutch manufacturing techniques and were thus different in detail to the uniforms made in Germany.

The Dutch SS man had to pay for his own uniform and boots.

As the Dutch SS uniform corresponded exactly with the German one described in detail in Volume 1 of this work, items will only be described insofar as they differ from the regulation German General SS service uniform.

SS DIENSTTUNIEK
SS Service tunic
As German.

SS RIJBROEK
SS Breeches
As German.

SS DIENSTKAPOTJAS
SS Service overcoat
As German.

SS DIENSTPET
SS Service peaked cap
As German but with a silver "Wolf Hook" (Wolfsangel) of the N.S.B. and W.A. in place of the SS eagle (Hoheitsabzeichen). There are cases where members of the Dutch SS wore the SS eagle, see "SS-Vormingsbladen" No. 6, 1944.

SS SCHOEISEL
SS Footwear
As German.

SS KLEDING
SS Underwear
Black shirt.
White shirt.
Black tie.

SS RANGAANDUIDINGEN
SS Badges of rank
The badges of rank in the Dutch SS corresponded exactly to those of the Allgemeine-SS. Although the official rank chart shows badges of rank for general officers, the most senior Dutch SS officer held the rank of SS-Standaardleider, and it is therefore presumed that they were never in fact required.

SS SPIEGELS
SS Collar patches
Collar patches were used to denote the rank and unit of the wearer. The unit designation was worn on the right, and the badge of rank on the left collar patch. The commander (Voorman) of the Dutch SS wore special collar patches as illustrated.
Members of the Staff of the Dutch SS wore a plain right hand collar patch.
Members of the numbered SS regiments (SS-Standaarden) wore the regimental number in Arabic in aluminium embroidery on the right collar patch. Collar patches were edged in twisted cord, according to rank (see Volume 1, p. 20).

SS-Rottenleider, Avegoor, August 1942.

(Above)   Commander of the 3rd regiment of the Dutch SS.

(Left)   Dutch SS man.

(opp. page)   Parade of the 1st Regiment of the Dutch SS.

Group of senior Dutch SS and police leaders, March 1943. Front row l. to r. Feldmeijer, Jansonius, unidentified SS leader, and Bettink. Back row. Two unidentified SS leaders, and three Dutch police officers.

SS RANGEN
SS Ranks

The ranks of the Dutch SS corresponded exactly with those of the Allgemeine-SS, but unlike those used by the Dutch Waffen-SS, were expressed in Dutch not German. The following is a comparison between Dutch SS and Allgemeine-SS ranks:

No.	NED.-SS/GERM. SS NED.	ALLGEMEINE-SS
1	SS-Maat	SS-Mann
2	SS-Stormman	SS-Sturmmann
3	SS-Rottenleider	SS-Rottenführer
4	SS-Onderschaarleider	SS-Unterscharführer
5	SS-Schaarleider	SS-Scharführer
6	SS-Opperschaarleider	SS-Oberscharführer
7	SS-Hoofdschaarleider	SS-Hauptscharführer
8	SS-Onderstormleider	SS-Untersturmführer
9	SS-Opperstormleider	SS-Obersturmführer
10	SS-Hoofdstormleider	SS-Hauptsturmführer
11	SS-Stormbanleider	SS-Sturmbannführer
12	SS-Opperstormbanleider	SS-Obersturmbannführer
13	SS-Standaardleider	SS-Standartenführer
14	SS-Opperleider	SS-Oberführer
15	SS-Brigadeleider	SS-Brigadeführer
16	SS-Groepsleider	SS-Gruppenführer
17	SS-Oppergroepsleider	SS-Obergruppenführer
18	Voorman	—

SS LEERWAREN
SS Leatherwear

Black leather belt and cross strap with two pronged nickel plated belt buckle and single pronged nickel plated cross strap buckle.

On June 23rd, 1942, Himmler issued an order back-dated to take effect on May 17th, permitting the Dutch SS to wear the German SS. belt buckle with motto "Meine Ehre heisst Treue"—Ref: Der Reichsführer-SS, Führerhauptquartier, den 23. Juni 1942, Tgb.Nr. RF/V.

PLATE 1
Dutch SS rank collar patches

PLATE 2
1. Shoulder cord for SS-Maat up to and incl. SS-Hoofdschaarleider.
2. Shoulder cord for SS-Onderstormleider up to and incl. SS-Hoofdstormleider.
3. Shoulder cord for SS-Stormbanleider up to and incl. Voorman.
4. Collar patches worn by the commander (Voorman) of the Dutch SS.

PLATE 3
1. Badge worn on the upper left arm by all members of the Dutch SS.
2. Badge worn on the upper left arm by SS departmental chiefs (Hoofden van Afdeelingen) and regimental commanders (Leiders van de Standaards) of the Dutch SS.
   (1, 2: Right half of inner triangle red.)
3. Badge worn on the upper right arm by all ranks in the Dutch SS. Here for commissioned ranks.
4. Armband worn by all members of the Dutch SS. (A report that members of the five SS regiments wore their regimental number in Arabic numerals on the armband, while only those of the staff and SS Police Regiment wore the plain band, is considered without foundation.)

PLATE 1

4

5

6

10

11

12

16

17

PLATE 2

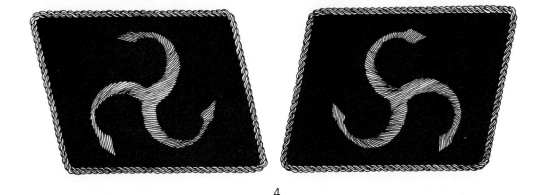

1   2   3

4

PLATE 3

1

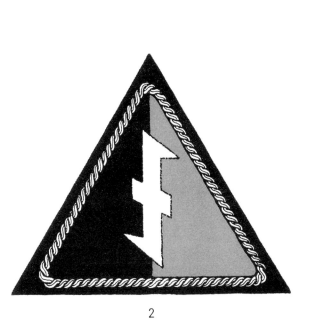

2

3

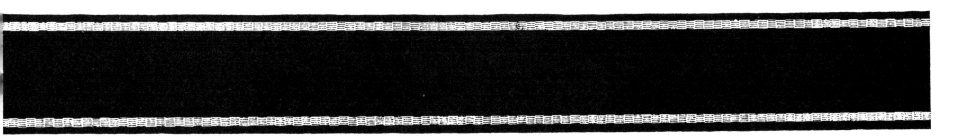

4

SS SPORT INSIGNES

SS Sports badges

Because of the importance attached to proficiency in sport, a number of awards were made to Dutch SS men at the SS School Avegoor in Ellecom. In the summer of 1941 a special award in four classes was introduced by Feldmeijer. August 9th., 1942, saw the first award of the Reichssportabzeichen to Dutch SS men, when one in gold, four in silver and two in bronze were issued. In April 1943 62 "Reichssportabzeichen" were presented, and finally in February 1944 95 "Germanische Leistungsrunen" were awarded to Dutchmen by Reichsführer-SS Heinrich Himmler.

The Dutch SS Sports Badge was awarded in three classes according to the age of the recipient.

In bronze for men between 20 and 30 years.

In silver for men between 30 and 42 years.

In gold for men of 42 years and older.

The Dutch SS Honour Sports Badge was awarded in gold only.

SS-Opperstormleider J. L. Jansonius (Chief-of-Staff of the Dutch SS) and a member of the Waffen-SS at a presentation ceremony of the "Reichssportabzeichen" at the SS School Avegoor, August 1942.

SS Sports badge (SS-Sportteeken).

SS Honour sports badge (SS-Sporteereteeken).

SS VLAG
SS Flag

The Dutch SS did not have unit flags or standards, but did carry a flag.

Dutch SS Flag.

HISTORY OF THE FLEMISH SS

Motto: Mijne Eer Is Trouw

The formation of the General SS in Belgium was complicated by various factors. In the first place for racial reasons it could not be representative of Belgium as a whole, but had to be drawn exclusively from the Flemings, for whereas they were considered sufficiently Germanic to be political SS men, the French-speaking Walloons were not. In fact as soon as Germany invaded Belgium on May 10th, 1940, it was made quite clear that for the purposes of occupation and collaboration the Flemings and the Walloons were to be treated separately and differently. For example, when in October 1940 Flemish P.O.W.s were released and allowed to return home to their families, their Walloon brothers-in-arms were not; and when Belgian volunteers stepped forward to serve with Germany against Bolshevism the Flemings were admitted into a unit of the SS (SS-Standarte "Westland", ordered by Hitler on May 25th, 1940, and made up of Flemish and Dutch volunteers), whereas the Walloons were formed into (as Himmler considered) a more lowly national legion serving with the German Army proper. In fact the Walloons were not admitted into the Waffen-SS until June 1st, 1943, when their Army Legion was upgraded to SS status as SS-Freiwilligen-Brigade "Wallonien".

Hitler's view, therefore, was that the Flemings were racially superior to the Walloons, and that they alone should be honoured with a national political SS formation. This was naturally very welcome to the more extremist Flemish collaborators, especially as Belgium had been dominated ever since its formation as a state in 1830 by the Walloon minority. From the beginning Flemings competed with Walloons and after the First World War Flemish veterans from the armed forces gathered together into groups striving for political equality. Most of these came from the veterans' association V.O.S. (Vlaamsche Oud Strijders), which although not a political party did wield considerable influence in Flemish nationalist circles and provided many of the future political leaders. Staf de Clercq, for example, who as will be seen below was

later to lead the Flemish equivalent to a Nazi party, belonged to the V.O.S. So did van Severen, who was to represent Italian Fascist thinking in the country.

The most important party to emerge in the early post-war years was the Frontpartij (Front Party). This was a highly nationalistic Flemish democratic political party, and although not restricted to war veterans was influenced to a certain extent by the V.O.S., which had provided many of its key figures.

In time extremists from the Frontpartij founded their own movements, and amongst these was one based on German National Socialism, and another on Italian Fascism. Staf de Clercq founded and led, until his death in October, 1942, the V.N.V. (Vlaamsche Nationaal Verbond), which until it started collaborating with the Germans during the Second World War was a democratic political party. It strove for an independent Flanders, had its own para-military organisation, and can be considered as the closest Flemish equivalent to a Nazi party. The Verdinaso, on the other hand, was based on Italian Fascism, was a movement rather than a political party, and so did not seek parliamentary representation. Rather it sought conquest of the so-called "State of the Lowlands" ("Dietsland"), comprising Holland, Belgium and the northern departments of France. The Verdinaso was prepared to achieve this conquest by any means, and its members are recorded as saying that this would have involved the use of force if necessary. It, too, had its own militia.

On May 10th, 1941, a part of the Verdinaso was amalgamated with the V.N.V., and the militias of both were fused together to form the "Dietsche Militie/Zwarte Brigade" (D.M./Z.B.).

Another movement existed with strong Nazi tendencies—the DeVlag (which although literally means "the Flag" was a contraction of the German "Deutsch-Vlämische Arbeitsgemeinschaft", which in Flemish is 'Vlaamsch-Duitsche Arbeidsgemeenschap"). This was formed with German support in 1935, and was led in Flanders by Dr. Jef Van de

Wiele. The DeVlag favoured annexation of Flanders to Germany and as such held views very different from the highly nationalistic de Clercq and his V.N.V. After 1940 the DeVlag met with increasing success and on 25th August 1943, Van de Wiele boasted 51,991 members. Professing to further cultural relations and build up friendship between Flanders and Germany, it had members in Germany (both Germans and Flemings) as well as in Belgium. It propagated the so-called "Germanic thought" preaching that Flemish-German political ties had to be as close as possible, but in point of fact sought the absorption of Flanders into a great German Reich. The DeVlag's headquarters in Germany were at Viktoria Luise Platz 1, Berlin W30, and in Brussels at Regentlaan 23, in the centre of the city and not far from the Gestapo's offices.

Van de Wiele, who held a doctorate in Germanic philology and was such a renowned drinker that he was known as "Jef-cognac" in SS circles, is claimed to have boasted that Hitler promised him the post of future Gauleiter of Flanders. True or false, there is little doubt that he would have been Germany's first choice in the event of an Axis victory, but if so, it is more likely that he would have been named "Volksführer" of Flanders, as Leon Degrelle would have been in Wallonia.

During occupation, therefore, the V.N.V. was not the only Nazi-style party in Flanders collaborating with the Germans, for the ideologically opposed DeVlag was also much in the fore. As a result, and because the aims of the V.N.V. differed from his own, when Himmler decided to establish a Flemish extension to the Allgemeine SS in late 1940 he did not make it a formation of the V.N.V. or any other party and it remained a separate entity throughout. Propaganda put out the idea of comradeship between the Flemish SS and the V.N.V., but this was far from the truth—great emnity existed between the two, they had no connection whatsoever, and in fact negotiations to include the Flemish SS as a formation of the V.N.V. ended in complete failure. The authority over the Flemish SS lay with the German SS representative R. Jungclaus (originally leader of SS-Abschnitt "Flandern", and after August 1st, 1944, Higher SS and Police Leader for the whole of Belgium), and no pretence was made, as in Holland and Norway, to have the local national SS subordinated to the local national Nazi leader.

As with the Dutch SS that had been formed shortly before, there was no fixed date of the foundation of the Flemish SS, nor was there any kind of official or even unofficial foundation ceremony. At the end of September 1940 about 80 men had been enrolled in Antwerp and another 50 in Ghent. Their official title from the beginning was "Algemeene SchutScharen Vlaanderen" or "Algemeene SS Vlaanderen", but they were also commonly referred to as "Algemeene Vlaamsche SS". just "Vlaamsche SS" and "SS-Vlaanderen". On September 1st, 1941, its entire strength was grouped together to form the First Flemish SS Regiment (1. SS-Standaard Vlaanderen, or 1. SS-Standarte Flandern), which was organised into four battalions totalling 18 companies. Those original members of the Flemish SS who were either unqualified or over the age of 35 were used to form an SS militia ("SS-Militie"), which on August 1st 1942, was renamed the "Flemish Corps" ("Vlaanderen-Korps", or "Flandern-Korps"). Little is known of this corps and it has been reported as both an SS reserve and a welfare association. Its ranks differed from the rest by having the German initials "FK—" used as a prefix rather than the usual "SS-".

On October 1st, 1942, the Flemish SS was renamed "Germanic SS (in) Flanders" ("Germaansche SS (in) Vlaanderen") to bring it in line with the other branches of the Germanic SS. Before that date, however, its membership had begun to decline heavily, with many volunteering for active service in the Waffen-SS, and so the head of the SS Main Office, Berger, came to depend more on the DeVlag than on the shrinking Flemish SS. In fact Berger was the president of the DeVlag with Jef Van de Wiele as "Landesleiter", or leader, in Flanders. Berger decided that Van de Wiele and his Flemish part of the DeVlag were better suited to his plans than the Flemish SS and he envisaged that DeVlag should eventually replace the V.N.V. and have the Flemish SS as its own militia. Actually DeVlag and the SS were closely interwoven and many Flemings belonged to both organisations. Another indication of the inter-relationship between Flemish SS and DeVlag is that according to the instructions for functionaries of the latter for service duties within that organisation men were required who were "members of the Germanic SS . . . or who can be considered as being on the same level". Once Berger switched his attention from the Flemish SS to the DeVlag the importance of the former diminished and DeVlag continued as the vehicle of SS ideology in Flanders. Eventually, in May 1944, the Flemish SS (including the Flemish Corps) was merged with DeVlag to form a "Security Corps" ("Sicherheitskorps"). By the autumn of that year it had virtually ceased to exist, and in September Belgium was liberated by the Allies.

The Flemish SS differed in several respects from its Dutch counterpart— whereas the Dutch SS was a formation of the N.S.B. the Flemish SS was in no way attached to the V.N.V., and whereas the Dutch SS had but one leader from beginning to end (or at least until his death), the Flemish SS had several leaders.

René Lagrou was the original commander of the Flemish SS, but in mid-February, 1941, at the age of 36, he left to join the "Germania" Regiment of the Waffen-SS. For some time he served on the Russian front as a war correspondent and is recorded as being the first Fleming to receive the second class Kriegsverdienstkreuz with swords. Wounded later that year he returned to Belgium, but did not resume his command of the Flemish SS. He remained a member, however, and in 1942/1943 was an SS-Hauptsturmführer in it, as well as being "Generale Sekretaris der

SS-Onderstormleider August Schollen.

Lapel badge for members of the Flemish SS for wear with civilian clothes.

Kommissie Rechtsherstel (Kommissie Borms)" (General Secretary of the Commission for Rehabilitation (Borms Commission)). In September, 1944, he flew to Germany and in 1945 was an officer in an SS police battalion.

Ir. J. E. de Langhe replaced Lagrou in either February or March, 1941, but when the First Flemish SS Regiment was established on September 1st of that year its commander was SS-Hauptsturmführer Raf van Hulse. The latter is reported as such even in the Christmas 1942 issue of the "DeVlag" magazine, but actually joined the Waffen-SS in August and was succeeded by Jef François, who was listed as leader of the Flemish SS in "DeVlag" of May, 1943.

Jef François had been the commander of the Verdinaso's militia (D.M.O.—Dinaso Militanten Orde) from 1937, and when part of this movement was amalgamated with the V.N.V. on May 10th, 1941, he was appointed a senior staff officer in the combined militia Dietsche Militie/Zwarte Brigade, and belonged to the V.N.V. for a time. In July 1941 he volunteered for service on the Russian front and attained the rank of SS-Untersturmführer in the Waffen-SS. A member of the Flemish SS, he succeeded van Hulse as its commander and has been reported as an "SS-Standartenführer" in that organisation, but whether this designated his actual rank, position, or both, is not known.

Although not a leader of the Flemish SS, one of its founder-members is worthy of mention in this study. This was Ward Hermans, who was one of the original members of Verdinaso until he quarelled with that movement's leader, van Severen. Leaving Verdinaso he joined the V.N.V., but yet again fell out with its leader, Staf de Clercq, and went off to help found the Flemish SS. This move may have been intended as a direct slight to his two former parties, and Hermans, in his new job as editor-in-chief of the Flemish SS newspaper "The SS Man" ("De SS Man"), went so far as to criticise the V.N.V. in public. In one article he remarked that the men of the Flemish SS had not taken long to decide what to do after the Belgian defeat in May 1940, which was a direct jab at the V.N.V. which had been hesitant to collaborate with the Germans.

Inspite of being a founder-member of the Flemish SS, Herman's subsequent role was but a minor one. He apparently soon lost interest in it and went off to Germany, where he broadcast propaganda to Flemish workers in the Reich from Bremen. He remained in considerable favour with the Nazi government which is demonstrated by the fact that he was able to pursuade Dr. Goebbels to prevent his fellow countryman Dr. Elias from being sent to the Dachau concentration camp (Elias had been the leader of the V.N.V. since Staf de Clercq's death in October, 1942).

SS-UNTERSTURMFÜHRER AUGUST SCHOLLEN

In addition to listing the various commanders of the Flemish SS and other key figures it is of interest to mention briefly in passing SS-Untersturmführer August Schollen. Born on September 11th, 1915, he took command of Stormban III/1. (i.e. the third Stormban, or battalion, of the first Standaard, or regiment) of the Germaansche SS in Vlaanderen and just three days later, on December 4th, 1942, was murdered in Brussels. Seizing upon the opportunity to create a young martyr/hero figure for the Flemish SS along the lines of Horst Wessel, the Flemish SS propaganda machine gave him considerable publicity. His funeral was held in Brussels on December 8th, 1942, and his photograph was published in various books and magazines of the time.

OPLEIDING
Training

The Flemish SS were trained at their own school at Schoten on the outskirts of Antwerp, which also served for French and Indian volunteers in the Waffen-SS. The school was named SS-Ausbildungslager Schoten, and was commanded from the beginning of 1943 until July of that year by SS-Hauptsturmführer Horst Schwertfeger, then by SS-Obersturmführer Rudel, and from July 1944 by SS-Sturmbannführer Lindemann.

Lapel badge for aiding members (B.L.) of the Flemish SS.

The funeral of SS-Onderstormleider August Schollen in Brussels on December 8th, 1942.

ORGANISATIE
Organisation

Originally the Flemish SS was not divided into sub-units as in Holland and Norway, and this was possibly due to its comparatively small size. On September 1st, 1941, all qualified members under the age of 35 went to form the First Flemish SS Regiment (1. SS-Standaard Vlaanderen, or 1. SS-Standarte Flandern), which was organised into 4 battalions, or Stormbannen (expressed in roman numerals) and 18 companies, or Stormen (arabic numerals), which in turn were subdivided into Troepen, etc., as in the Dutch SS (see page 9). Those insufficiently qualified, or over the age of 35, were formed into the SS Militia (SS-Militie), which on August 1st, 1942, was renamed the Flemish Corps (Vlaanderen-Korps, or Flandern-Korps). Theoretically a second and even a third SS regiment followed, and although they are believed to have been undermanned as a result of Waffen-SS recruitment, it is known that a 3rd SS Regiment was in existence by mid-1942 (see "De SS Man", No. 27, June 13th, 1942 : "De 3e SS-Standaard"). If these did in fact exist they should have been subdivided as the First, but almost certainly were not in view of the shortage of men. This factor also created the situation whereby so-called battalions were led by officers of low rank, or even by NCOs.

In May, 1944, the Flemish SS and Flemish Corps were merged with the DeVlag to form a Security Corps (Sicherheitskorps).

To arrive at a total membership figure for the Flemish SS is almost impossible, due to the constant movement of men from one organisation to another and the lack of detailed information. In the autumn of 1941, for example, there were some 1,800 members. By June 30th, 1944, the total strength had risen to 3,499 men, but as 501 of these were in the Flemish Corps, 1660 in the Waffen-SS and 939 in other organisations such as the NSKK, Org. Todt, Org. Speer and German Navy, the effective number still in the Flemish SS (including 98 probationary members) was only 399. Another report, of July 1944, gives 803 members, but lacks details of composition.

The Flemish SS is reported to have contained a youth section named the "Youth Front", which was forced to amalgamate with the N.S.J.V. (the V.N.V. youth movement). Flemish youths inclined towards the SS but too young to join are reported to have favoured the De Vlag's" Hitler-jeugd Vlaanderen" ("Flemish Hitler Youth"), which was a bitter opponent of the N.S.J.V.

The Headquarters of the Flemish SS (Hoofdkwartier der Algemeene SS) was in Antwerp, at Mechelsche Steenweg 204.

BESCHERMENDE LEDEN
Aiding members

In common with the Allgemeine SS in Germany and the other branches of the Germanic SS in Holland and Norway, it was possible for Flemings to contribute funds to the Flemish SS without actually becoming full members. These contributions were based on a monthly minimum and in return one received a silver lapel badge numbered on the reverse. Such aiding or, by direct translation, protecting, members were called "Beschermende Leden" ("B.L.") and their lapel badge consisted of these letters placed on either side of silver SS runes as illustrated on page 25.

FIRST PATTERN UNIFORM

From its foundation in December 1940 until at least May 9th, 1941, the Flemish SS wore a uniform similar to the early German SS "Traditionsanzug", which consisted of brown shirt, black tie, black breeches, and black leather belt, cross strap and boots. At a march past in May 1941 in Ghent, the entire formation (then known as 1. SS-Standaard Vlaanderen) wore this simple uniform. Only its commander SS-Hauptsturmführer Raf van Hulse wore a cap, and this was a black field cap with a silver or white inverted chevron on the front containing either a button or death's head. No insignia appears to have been worn on this uniform, nor is it known how the rank of the wearer was indicated. The belt buckle was the two pronged type as used by the Dutch SS.

THE BLACK SS SERVICE UNIFORM

In common with the other three branches of the Germanic SS the Flemings were eventually issued with a black SS service uniform of German manufacture. As the Flemish SS uniform corresponded exactly with the German one described in Volume 1 of this work, items will only be described insofar as they differ from the regulation German

General SS uniform.

SS DIENSTTUNIEK
SS Service tunic
As German.

SS RIJBROEK
SS Breeches
As German.

SS DIENSTKAPOTJAS
SS Service overcoat
As German.

SS DIENSTPET
SS Service peaked cap
As German but with a silver diamond-shaped swastika in place of the SS eagle (Hoheitsabzeichen).

SS VELDMUTS
SS Field cap
Black cloth field cap with silver button in front, and the diamond-shaped swastika on the left side.

SS SCHOEISEL
SS Footwear
As German.

SS HANDSCHOENEN
SS Gloves
White cloth.

SS ONDERGOED
SS Underwear
Brown shirt.
Black tie.

SS RANGDISTINCTIEVEN
SS Badges of rank
It is presumed that the Flemish SS used the same badges of rank and titles as the Dutch SS.

No rank higher than the equivalent to the German "SS-Standartenführer" has been found.

SS KRAAGDISTINCTIEVEN
SS Collar patches
Collar patches were used to denote the rank and unit of the wearer. The unit designation was worn on the right, and the badge of rank on the left collar patch.

Members of the staff of the Flemish SS wore a plain right hand collar patch.

Members of the SS regiments wore the regimental number in aluminium embroidered arabic numerals on the right collar patch.

SS DIENSTDOLK
SS Service dagger
German SS daggers were in some cases worn by members of the Flemish SS, and officers also wore a knot.

SS LEERWAREN
SS Leatherwear
Black leather belt with either the nickel plated two pronged pattern, or special Flemish SS buckle. The German SS belt buckle is believed to have been introduced for all ranks in mid-1942—in any case it is known to have been worn by certain officers. The belt was worn with a black leather cross strap with aluminium slide buckle of German manufacture.

Flemish SS Flag.

PLATE 4

1. Badge worn on the upper left arm by all ranks in the Flemish SS. Here for non-commissioned ranks.
2. Flemish SS other ranks belt buckle.
3. Armband for all ranks of the Flemish SS.
4. Armband for all ranks of the Flemish Corps.

PLATE 4

1

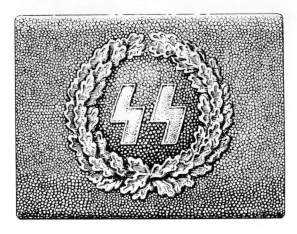

2

3

4

Reichscommissar for occupied Norway Terboven, Higher SS and Police Leader Rediess and Vidkun Quisling, February 1942.

HISTORY OF THE NORWEGIAN SS
Motto: Min Ære er Troskap

Germany invaded Norway on April 9th, 1940, and in September of that year Josef Terboven was appointed Reichscommissar. Under him and representing the SS in occupied Norway came a "Higher SS and Police Leader", at first SS-Obergruppenführer und General der Polizei Weitzel, but soon after replaced by SS-Obergruppenführer und General der Polizei Wilhelm Rediess ("Der Höhere SS- und Polizeiführer beim Reichskommissar für die besetzten norwegischen Gebiete").

Vidkun Abraham Lauritz Quisling (born 1887) was the Norwegian Minister of Defence in the Agrarian Government, but when this fell in 1933 he formed a fascist-style political party called the Nasjonal Samling ("N.S."—"National Union"). This party with its para-military troops the Hird (similar to the S.A. of the N.S.D.A.P. in Germany) was consequently in existence when the Germans invaded. Quisling was believed to have been a party to the German invasion, and the regime he proclaimed upon their arrival so incensed the Norwegian people that it lasted only a week. Quisling still continued to lead his Nasjonal Samling, however, which was the only political party permitted in Norway by the occupying forces. Reichscommissar Terboven was extremely hostile to Quisling and as unco-operative as possible, but on Hitler's orders did help him to build up the strength of the N.S. The success of Quisling's efforts can be seen from the increase in N.S. membership from 6,000 in September 1940 to its peak of between 45,000 and 60,000 in early 1943. Under occupation the Nasjonal Samling grew and with it the Hird, which was by then outfitted with uniforms and insignia similar to the German S.A. There was, however, no Norwegian political SS organization such as already had been formed in Holland and Flanders, as Quisling was very much against the idea. For despite his shortcomings, Quisling was fanatically pro-Norwegian and he rightly saw in the political SS a movement towards a Great German Reich, and a threat to Norway of being incorporated into it as a mere district (Gau). But whereas Quisling was against the formation of a Norwegian political SS, Himmler, his "Higher

SS and Police Leader", Rediess, and Reichscommissar Terboven were strongly in favour of it.

Quisling and Terboven fought bitterly and the latter did all in his power to diminish the importance of Quisling and his Nasjonal Samling. One of Terboven's attempts was even to replace Quisling as "Fører" (leader) of the N.S. in June 1940 by his old friend from the Saar, Chief of Police Jonas Lie (born 1899), who although not a member of the party was a strong sympathizer. It was only through the diplomacy of one of Quisling's best friends, Albert Viljam Hagelin, that the plan failed for Hagelin stated (quite without foundation) that Quisling had appointed him as deputy leader of the N.S. and that he should therefore take over the leadership and not Lie.

This rivalry between Terboven and Quisling continued and in mid-1941 Terboven and Lie once again got together and set about the formation of a Norwegian political SS contingent behind Quisling's back. According to subsequent N.S. propaganda it was at a meeting of the 7th Hird Regiment "Viking" in Oslo on May 16th, 1941, that the creation of such a unit was first suggested, and it was a suggestion that apparently met with some enthusiasm, for a number of the Hird men present declared themselves willing to join at once. They had not long to wait, for just one week later (on May 21st, 1941) a Norwegian political SS formation was established and called "Norway's SS" ("Norges SS"). On that day Reichsführer-SS Heinrich Himmler flew in to Oslo where he was met by Reichscommissar Terboven, a disgruntled Quisling, and a number of senior SS and Wehrmacht officers, and then taken to the Nasjonal Samling's Party House.

The ceremony opened with a speech by the Rikshird's Chief of Staff, Orvar Sæther, who spoke to his former Hird men that had volunteered to be the first aspirants of the new Norwegian SS. He explained how they were about to join SS comrades from all the other Germanic

Jonas Lie and members of the Norwegian SS, May 1941.

Members of the Norwegian SS swear the oath of allegiance to Hitler and Quisling, May 1941.

countries, and how their role was to protect and safeguard the future of the Germanic race.

Once Sæther had handed over his Hird men to the SS, Heinrich Himmler took the stand and described to them the development of the SS in Germany from its establishment in 1925 until the present day, and also how the SS stood as a guarantee for the future of the Germanic communities. Having referred to the achievements of the Norwegian volunteers in the SS-Regiment "Nordland" (then serving with the "Wiking" division of the Waffen-SS) which had been raised in January 1941 from Norwegian and Danish volunteers, Himmler stated that the formation of the Norges SS was a new and important step forward for the Germanic community. The honour for its foundation, he told his audience, would fall upon Norway.

Himmler then appointed cabinet minister and Norwegian Chief of Police Jonas Lie as SS-standartfører and leader of the Norwegian SS (as has been seen above, Lie was an old friend of Terboven, and had been chosen by him to found and recruit for the Norwegian SS—Lie was a sympathizer of the N.S. but not a party member and was a man disliked and distrusted by Quisling). The oath of allegiance was taken by Lie, who then administered it to his men, and was given to both Hitler and Quisling.

Immediately after the ceremony the new SS aspirants travelled to the SS school at Elverum, where they received a beginners' course lasting six weeks.

To sum up, although the Norwegian SS was created as a subdivision of the Nasjonal Samling it was strongly opposed by Quisling, and recruiting by Jonas Lie was at first carried on behind Quisling's back, and later in direct defiance to his orders. Loyal N.S. members were urged to oppose Lie's recruiting drive and this met with partial success at first, but the Norwegian SS was too strongly backed by both Lie's State Police and Terboven's Reichscommissariat to be blocked in this way. Whether

Quisling liked it or not, and he certainly did not, the political SS had arrived in Norway and there it was to stay until the very end of the war. On May 11th, 1941, the Department of Justice issued an order in which it outlined the rights the participant in the SS had with respect to his previous civilian work and his pay in civilian life.

On June 22nd, 1941, Germany and her allies attacked the Soviet Union and the Norwegian SS was presented with an ideal opportunity to further its anti-Communist and pan-Germanic convictions. Upon the declaration of war with Russia some 85% of the Norwegian SS under sveitfører Captain Berg, as well as their leader Jonas Lie, volunteered for the Norwegian Volunteer SS Legion ("Frw. Legion 'Norwegen'", or "Den norske Legion"), and almost all were eventually promoted to officer or N.C.O. rank. (NOTE: Some confusion existed in contemporary Norwegian publications as to the exact number of Norwegian SS men that volunteered for the Legion. Of the original 130 members—and one report even gives this as 151—some sources state that 85% joined, whereas others give 85 men.) The Norwegian SS thereby provided five company commanders, one of whom had been killed and two wounded before the end of 1943. In fact the majority of the leaders of the Legion were drawn from the Norwegian SS.

On February 1st, 1942, Vidkun Quisling was appointed Minister President of Norway, and his personal power and that of his Nasjonal Samling and its para-military organizations was increased from that date, for he was no longer the leader of a political party tolerated by the Germans—he was the leader of the Norwegian Government.

Fourteen months after its establishment the title "Norges SS" was altered on July 21st, 1942, to "Germanske SS Norge" ("Germanic SS Norway") by a Party Order signed by Quisling. This document is worthy of full translation:

"**Party Order** of the Germanic SS Norway dated July 21st, 1942.

On May 21st, 1941, the "Norges SS" was established. In addition to the rules and regulations laid down at the time the following new rules and regulations are established:

1. The name "Norges SS" shall be changed to "Germanske SS Norge".
2. "Germanske SS Norge" is a National Socialist military organization which shall consist of men of Nordic race and mentality. It is an independent subdivision of the Nasjonal Samling, which is directly subordinated to the N. S. Fører (leader of the N.S., i.e. Quisling) and is responsible to him. It is at the same time a subdivision of the Greater Germanic SS and shall contribute its part to pointing out before the Germanic people the road to a new future and create the foundation for a Germanic peoples' association.
3. The following may be accepted as members of the "Germanske SS Norge" if they otherwise comply with the conditions covering membership in the SS:
   a) male members of the Nasjonal Samling
   b) Norwegian citizens who have served at least one year in the Waffen-SS or in the Norwegian Volunteer Legion ("Den norske Legion")
   c) other Norwegian citizens provided that the General Secretariat of the Nasjonal Samling approves their application.
4. The transfer of the various subdivisions and special organizations of the Nasjonal Samling to the "Germanske SS Norge" or vice versa may be effected to the extent as may be deemed necessary. In any event the consent of the Fører to the special organization or subdivision must be secured covering the proposed transfer.
5. Members of the SS cannot at the same time belong to the Rikshird or NSUF. An exception to this rule is made in regard to Party officials and leaders in the mentioned special organizations.

Oslo, July 21st, 1942.
(Signed) Quisling
R. J. FUGLESANG (signed)"

Apart from the racial and political requirements, volunteers for the Germanske SS Norge had to be between 17 and 40 years of age and not less than 1.70 meters in height.

It is interesting to note that the formation of the Norwegian political SS, in contrast to the other three branches of the Germanic SS, paralleled on the surface at least that of the Allgemeine-SS in Germany, for the SS in both cases was an élite force created within—and later taken from—the original party para-military organization (the S.A. in Germany and the Hird in Norway). Evidence of the strong connections between Hird and Norwegian SS can be found in the fact that for some time they shared the same newspaper—"Hirdmannen" ("The Hird Man"). For from the issue dated May 24th, 1941, to that of April 4th, 1942, "Hirdmannen' was sub-titled "—Kamporgan for Rikshird og Norges SS' ("—combat journal for the National Hird and the Norwegian SS"). It was over a year after the formation of the Norwegian SS that they founded their own newspaper, and the first issue of "Germaneren—Kamporgan for Gemanske SS Norge" appeared on July 25th, 1942.

As the war progressed and the Axis powers' chances of victory faded the Norwegian SS was used more as a front line formation than the political organization that it had been intended for. It has been seen that as Germany went to war with the Soviet Union the majority of the original members of the Norwegian SS volunteered for service in the Norwegian Volunteer Legion—this was to be the first of many such contributions. On March 11th, 1943, members of the Germanske SS Norge joined SS-Panzer-Grenadier-Regiment "Norge". Soon afterwards the Germanske SS Norge formed a full company of their own to fight on the Eastern Front, and this paraded before Quisling on May 6th, 1943, under the command of SS-Obersturmführer and Deputy Leader of the Germanske SS Norge Olaf Lindvig (he had been appointed as such on March 13th, 1943). On May 20th, 1943, Jonas Lie was awarded the SS-Totenkopfring by Himmler. On August 16th, 1943, after the "SS Day in Oslo" (SS-Dagen, 14th-15th August) Quisling spoke to units of the Norwegian SS on parade at Slottsplassen, and on the following day (August 17th) the Norwegian SS, together with the Police, National Hird and Quisling's bodyguard (Førergard) were integrated into the Norwegian armed forces. (NOTE: According to Keesing's the law was dated August 14th, 1943).

The total strength of the Norwegian SS at September 30th, 1944 was 1,247, of which 330 were at the front, 245 in the police, and 511 in emergency units. Thus the Norwegian SS then consisted of only 161 men, but with 3,422 Aiding Members ("S.M.") and 9,137 subscribers to their newspaper "Germaneren".

For some time Himmler thought that Lie was leading the Norwegian SS in a somewhat disinterested manner and was not giving this task the attention and devotion it deserved. He therefore replaced Lie on January 1st, 1945, by Sverre Riisnæs.

On March 1st, 1945, Olaf Lindvig (then an SS-Hauptsturmführer) again took up the post of Chief of Staff of the Norwegian SS ("Stabsleder G.SS.N"), which had previously been held by Leif Schjøren.

In May 1945 Norway was liberated by the Allies, and the German capitulation was broadcast on the 7th. Two days later Terboven and Rediess drank large quantities of akevitt and beer and committed suicide by sitting down on a land mine in a bunker on the Crown Prince's property. Jonas Lie also consumed more akevitt than was good for

Lapel badge worn with civilian dress by members of the **Norwegian SS**.

him, for it induced a heart-attack and he died of malarial shock. Vidkun Quisling declined offers of escape and, unlike Terboven, Rediess and Lie, refused to commit suicide and stood trial for treason. He was executed on October 24th, 1945.

OPPLÆRING
Training

SS-Skole Elverum was opened on the day of the foundation of the Norwegian SS, May 21st, 1941, and the first batch of volunteer aspirants went there directly for a six weeks' course. In August 1942 the Kongsvinger Fortress was opened as a school for the Germanske Norge and in that month forty-two recruits were admitted. The course lasted four weeks and the instruction comprised both military and political subjects. On October 16th, 1942, more SS men were admitted to what is assumed to have been the second course. In December 1942 a third course was held which was subdivided into three parts, comprising a short course for front line soldiers; a non-commissioned officers' course for SS men; and a recruiting course. An officer from Vest-Opland named K. Sveen was in charge of these courses.

While not actually attending training courses members of the Norwegian SS continued their normal civilian activities. They were trained within their local SS-Storm during off-hours each Wednesday evening and every second Sunday.

In 1942 a riding school for the Germanske SS Norge ("SS-Rideskolen") was opened in Oslo at Drammensvegen 1. It was commanded by Major Henschien and a Herr Dryander was "Leiter des Rennstalles". Based upon this SS riding school a cavalry section of the Norwegian SS was formed under Major Henschien with twenty horses. In September 1942 a riding meeting for Norwegian and German SS was held at Porsgrunn, and Major Henschien, Captain Waksvik, Bernt Anker and Dryander took part. Mention has also been found of the "Norges Rideskole" at Vinderen (Hippodromen), in connection with the Germanske SS Norge.

SS SCHOOLS: a) SS-Skole Elverum
                 b) SS-Skole Kongsvinger Festning
                 c) SS-Rideskole, Drammensvegen 1, Oslo
                 d) Norges Rideskole, Vinderen (Hippodromen), Oslo

ORGANISASJON
Organization

The complexity of the Staff of the Norwegian SS at first increased as the organization itself grew and eventually decreased as the war drew to a close and more desk-bound members were called to the front. To illustrate this fact the organization of the Staff is set out below at three different dates:

1942:

KONTOR: Office:	Drammensvegen 1, Oslo
SJEF: Commander:	Minister Jonas Lie, Akersgt. 44, Oslo
STEDFORTREDER: Substitute:	SS-stormfører O. Lindvik

Ref. "N. S. Årbok 1942", published 1943, p. 40.

1943:

SJEF: Commander:	SS-standartfører Jonas Lie
HOVEDSTABEN: H.Q. Staff:	Oslo, Drammensvegen 105
STABSLEDER: Chief of Staff:	Leif Schjøren
ADJUTANT: Adjutant:	SS-stormfører Hallvard Svelle
PRESSE- OG PROPAGANDA: Press & Propaganda:	SS-neststandartfører Sverre Riisnæs
ORGANISASJONSAVDELINGEN: Organization Section:	SS-stormfører Hallvard Svelle
ØKONOMIAVDELINGEN: Economics Section:	SS-mann, advokat Arne Schultz
PERSONALAVDELINGEN:	SS-lagfører Karl G. Blomfeldt

Personnel Section:

STABSLÆGEN: **Staff Doctor:**	SS-neststormfører Johan Fasting
IDRETTSLEDEREN: **Sport Leader:**	SS-nestlagfører Bertel Paaske
FORVALTNINGSLEDEREN: **Administration Leader:**	SS-nestlagfører Rolf Woye Pedersen
KULTUR OG RADIO: **Culture & Radio:**	SS-nesttroppfører Karl Aagaard(-)Østvig
JURIDISK RÅDGIVER: **Legal Consultant:**	SS-nesttroppfører, høyesterettsdommer Arvid Vasbotten
"GERMANEREN" OG SKOLEHEFTENE: **"Germaneren" & school journals:**	SS-nestlagfører Egil Holst Torkildsen
STØTTENDE MEDLEMMER: **Aiding members:**	Mari Selle
NORGES RIDESKOLE: **Norwegian Riding School:**	Vinderen (Hippodromen), Oslo
"GERMANEREN":	Akersgaten 8, Oslo
SS-SKOLE: **SS-School:**	Kongsvinger Festning (Fortress)

Ref. "N. S. Årbok 1944", published 1943, p. 72.

NOTE: In addition to the above, the following relevant entries are to be found in "Germaneren" dated January 30th, 1943:

HOVEDKONTORET: **Head Office:**	Colbjørnsensgt. 1
SS-RIDESKOLEN: **SS Riding School:**	Drammensvegen 1

1945:

HOVEDSTABEN: **H.Q. Staff:**	Drammensvegen 105, Oslo
STABSLEDER **Chief of Staff**	
ADJUTANT **Adjutant**	
ORGANISASJONSAVDELINGEN **Organization Section**	
PERSONALAVDELINGEN **Personnel Section**	
ØKONOMIAVDELINGEN **Economics Section**	
STABSLÆGEN **Staff Doctor**	
IDRETTSLEDEREN **Sport Leader**	
FORVALTNINGSLEDEREN **Administration Leader**	
RESEPSJONEN **Reception**	
"Germaneren":	Akersgt. 8, Oslo
SS-SKOLEN **SS School**	Kongsvinger Festning (Fortress)

Ref. "Nasjonal Samling Telefonliste og Adressebok", Januar 1945

DISTRICT ORGANIZATION

The Norwegian SS was subdivided into units in exactly the same manner as the Allgemeine-SS in Germany, but of course on a much smaller scale, and a comparison between the two can be seen from the following chart:

Germanske SS Norge	Allgemeine-SS	English Equivalent
Standart	Standart	Regiment
Stormbann/Fylking	Sturmbann	Battalion
Storm	Sturm	Company
Tropp	Trupp	Platoon
Lag	Schar	Squad
Rode	Rotte	File

The following comments can be made on the units of the Norwegian SS:

Standart: Although the rank of SS-standartfører was held, there do not appear to have been any units of this size in the Norwegian SS.

Stormbann: Also referred to as a Fylking, only one is recorded and that SS-Stormbann Oslo-Akershus (possibly the result of a fusion of SS-Storm Oslo with SS-Storm Akershus). Theoretically an SS-Stormbann could contain up to 4 SS-Stormer.

Storm: The basic local unit of the Norwegian SS which was established as a volunteer unit. It was commanded by an SS-Stormfører and carried the name of the district. Late in the war an attempt was made to number each SS-Storm and that of Greater Oslo received the number "1". The others, however, do not appear to have been so numbered. The SS-Storm contained 3 or 4 Tropper and combined all the units of a Fylke.

Tropp: The Tropp was commanded by a Troppfører and although in theory it could contain 3 or 4 Lag, in practice it contained only 3. It was arranged that the leader of the Tropp and the leaders of the subordinate Lag should as far as possible live in the same district.

Lag: Commanded by a Lagfører who should, as far as possible, live in the same district as his Troppfører. It contained 9 men.

Rode: 3 men.

As with the complexity of the Staff organization, that of the district units increased as the Norwegian SS grew and decreased as the war came to an end and its members were drawn into the Waffen-SS, or killed. Thus SS-Stormer that are listed in 1943 were reduced to non-specified formations or had ceased to exist at all by 1945. The situation was aggravated further by the reorganisation of the N.S. districts on October 29th, 1943. Below is a composite listing of all recorded local units:

SS-STORMBANN OSLO-AKERSHUS

Possibly the successor formation of both SS-Storm 1, Stor Oslo, and SS-Storm Akershus, it was listed in January 1943. Its address was Drammensvegen 1, Oslo.

SS-STORMER
SS Companies

SS-STORM SS-Company	NS FYLKESORGANISASJON NS District	SS-STORMFØRER Company Commander	ADRESS Address
1*	—	—	—
AGDER†	F.O. 9 Agder	?	Ostre Strandgt. 61
AKERSHUS	F.O. 1 Aust-Viken	Gunnar Theodorsen Emil Bruun Evers	?
AUST-AGDER†	F.O. 9 Agder	Trygve Gårbo (fung.)	?
BERGEN‡	—	—	—

BUSKERUD	F.O. 3 Vest-Viken	Peter Thomas Sandborg	Haugesgt. 17, Drammen
		Dagfinn Henriksen (fung.)	
HEDMARK§	F.O. 4 Hedmark	Sverre Lie	Grønnegt. 1, Hamar
HORDALAND‡	F.O. 12 Bergen og Hordaland	Richard Clason	?
MØRE OG ROMSDAL	F.O. 15 Møre og Romsdal	Frithjof Sanner	?
NORDLAND	F.O. 18 Nordland	Eilif Spjeldnes	?
NORD-TRØNDELAG	F.O. 17 Nord-Trøndelag	Hans Petter Hoff/Knut Solberg	?
		Kristian Solem (fung.)	
OPLAND§	F.O. 4 Hedmark og Opland	Sverre Lie	?
	F.O. 5 Opland		
OSLO*	F.O. 2 Stor-Oslo	Arne Juel Odde	Drammensvegen 105
		Kjell Kracht	Oslo
		Hallvard Svelle	
ROGALAND	F.O. 11 Rogaland	Olav. B. Haugland	Kongsgt. 18
STOR-OSLO*	—	—	—
SØR-TRØNDELAG	F.O. 16 Sør-Trøndelag	Hans Petter Hoff/Knut Solberg	?
		Sverre Klungtveit (fung.)	
TELEMARK	F.O. 8 Telemark	Arne Stridsklev (fung.)	Hesselberggaten 2, Skien
VEST-AGDER†	F.O. 9 Agder	Mathias Jacobsen	?
VESTFOLD	F.O. 3 Vest-Viken	Herman Bay	Kammegt. 4, Tønsberg
		Halvor Nygård	
ØSTFOLD	F.O. 1 Aust-Viken	Gunnar Lindblom	?

*SS-Storm Oslo was eventually renamed SS-Storm 1, Stor-Oslo (Greater Oslo), and at times was known as SS-Storm Stor-Oslo. It was the first formed SS company and was originally commanded by Police Lieutenant Arne Juel Odde. It contained 3 Tropper.

†At one time there was just one SS company in N.S. District 9, called "Agder"; at another there were two—"Aust-Agder" and "Vest-Agder".

‡The name "Bergen" appeared on an SS company flag (see p. 49), yet although Norway's second largest town, no company has been found bearing this name. The 12th N.S. District included Bergen and Hordaland, and although the SS company formed there carried the second name, the first appears to have been used on the flag.

§Originally N.S. District 4 included both Hedmark and Opland, but in accordance with the regional reorganisation law of October 29th, 1943, Opland was made into a separate District and numbered 5.

NOTE: The 13th, 19th and 20th N.S. Districts appear never to have contained formations of the Norwegian SS.

STØTTENDE MEDLEMMER
Aiding members

Norwegians were able to become aiding members of the Germanske SS Norge ("Støttende Medlemmer" or "S.M.") and in return for their minimum monthly contribution of one Kroner to the funds of the Norwegian SS they were given a silver and black enamel pin bearing their "S.M." number on the reverse. The total number of Norwegian aiding members is not known, but there were 3,422 of them on the 30th September 1944. Their representative on the Staff of the Norwegian SS was Mari Selle.

Lapel badge for Aiding Members (S.M.) of the Norwegian SS.

THE FIRST PATTERN UNIFORM

The 130 volunteers for the Norwegian SS that assembled at the Nasjonal Samling's Party House on May 21st, 1941, wore German Army field grey uniforms, with German SS belts, Hird shoulder straps and brassards. None of the volunteers wore collar patches. The newness of the shoulder straps suggest that they were specially made in one batch and issued with the uniforms, and it is therefore probable that while they followed the style of the Hird rank strap, they used white and silver piping and braid in place of red and gold. Jonas Lie wore shoulder straps of a Hird regimental commander (Regimentfører) which corresponded with his new appointment as SS-standartfører of the Norwegian SS.

Lie wore a field grey SS leaders' cap with the SS version of the national emblem (Hoheitsabzeichen) replaced by the emblem of the Nasjonal Samling ("Solørn", or "N.S.-riksørn"). The volunteers wore field grey field caps with a white metal button in front (which may have had the skull on it) and the emblem of the Nasjonal Samling, machine embroidered in grey silk on a black cloth base, on the left side.

This uniform was worn until replaced on, or shortly before September 25th, 1942, by the black service uniform of the German General SS.

THE BLACK SERVICE UNIFORM

Worn in public for the first time on September 25th, 1942, this uniform corresponded exactly with that worn by the German General SS, and may even have been of German manufacture. The Norwegian uniform will be described only insofar as it differs from the German one. A certain national identity was retained by the Norwegian SS in the wearing of the mountain instead of the peaked cap. The German mountain cap which they adopted was very similar to the cap of the Norwegian Army, which is still worn today.

SS TJENESTE JAKKE
SS Service tunic
As German.

SS TJENESTE VÅPENFRAKK
SS Service overcoat
As German.

SS RIDEBUKSE
SS Breeches
As German.

SS SKIBUKSE
SS Ski trousers
As well as black breeches, the Norwegian SS wore long black trousers as issued to the General SS for skiing (see Volume 1, p. 63). These had two slanting side pockets with buttoned flaps, a watch pocket and two back pockets with buttoned flaps. The trousers were fastened at the ankle.

SS SKYGGELUE
SS Ski cap
Unlike the other three branches of the Germanic SS and the General SS itself, the Norwegian SS were not issued with a peaked cap, but wore a black cloth ski cap (referred to as the "alpejegermodell") on all occasions. Black cloth cap with matching peak and flap fastened in front with two small white metal buttons. The only badge on this cap was the woven silk skull worn in front. Leaders seem to have worn the same cap as the other ranks.

SS STÅLHJELM
SS Steel helmet

The German 1935 model steel helmet sprayed black was used by the Norwegian SS, and it also appears that the field grey German Army helmets complete with the Army eagle (Hoheitsabzeichen) were worn as issued.

SS SKOTØY
SS Footwear

    Black boots
    Black lace-up ankle boots
    Black lace-up ski boots
    Black lace-up shoes

SS HANSKER
SS Gloves

    Black leather
    White cloth

SS UNDERTØY
SS Underwear

    Brown shirt
    White shirt
    Black tie

SS LÆRTØY
SS Leatherwear

Black leather belt and cross strap with nickel plated two pronged belt buckle and single pronged cross strap buckle. The German SS belt and buckle is also known to have been worn, and as it was referred to as the "belt buckle for the whole Germanic SS" in an order from Himmler dated June 23rd, 1942, it may have been introduced for the entire Germanic SS about that time.

SS TJENESTE DOLK
SS Service dagger

The Chief of Staff of the Norwegian SS is known to have worn the 1936 model SS service dagger. An example with the Norwegian version of the SS civilian badge on the top of the grip does exist.

SS-standartfører Jonas Lie (here just back from the Eastern Front and in Waffen-SS uniform), with members of the Norwegian SS and Police, March 1943.

SS DISTINKSJONER
SS Badges of rank

From the date of foundation on May 21st, 1941, until the introduction in September 1942 of the German SS system, Hird rank insignia was worn. Following the Hird system, badges of rank appeared on both shoulder straps only and consisted of silver braid bars of different widths for commissioned, and white tape bars of different widths for non-commissioned ranks. From September 1942 the Norwegian SS wore German SS badges of rank.

SS KOMMANDOSPEIL
SS Collar patches

Rank was shown on the left collar patch in the usual way, but all ranks wore the circular swastika ("SS-solhjulet"—literally "SS sun wheel") on the right patch. Thus the unit within the Norwegian SS was not shown on the right collar patch as in the Dutch and Flemish branches, but then this is not surprising as the Norwegian SS never constituted a full regiment. The Chief of Staff of the Norwegian SS ("Stabsleder i GSSN") held no official rank and wore the circular swastika on both collar patches.

SS GRADER
SS Ranks

The final ranks of the Norwegian SS were based on those of the German General SS, but unlike those of the Norwegian Waffen-SS they were expressed in Norwegian and not German. At first the Norwegian SS used the rank insignia of the Hird (from which it was formed) and it is therefore possible that they used the same titles. The following chart compares Hird and Norwegian SS rank titles with those of the German General SS. Rank titles were exact translations (although a little out of sequence) into Norwegian of the original German. But unlike the ranks of the General SS those of the Norwegian SS did not start with a capital letter.

No.	HIRD	NORGES SS/GSSN	ALLGEMEINE-SS
1	Hirdmann	SS-mann	SS-Mann
2	Nestspeider	SS-stormmann	SS-Sturmmann
3	Speider	SS-rodefører	SS-Rottenführer
4	Nestlagfører	SS-nestlagfører	SS-Unterscharführer
5	Lagfører	SS-lagfører	SS-Scharführer
6	Kommandersersjant/Furer	SS-nesttroppfører	SS-Oberscharführer
7	Troppfører	SS-troppfører	SS-Hauptscharführer
8	Nestsveitfører	SS-neststormfører	SS-Untersturmführer
9	Sveitfører	SS-stormfører	SS-Obersturmführer
10	—	SS-høvedsmann	SS-Hauptsturmführer
11	Fylkingfører	SS-stormbannfører	SS-Sturmbannführer
12	Nestregimentfører	SS-neststandartfører	SS-Obersturmbannführer
13	Regimentfører	SS-standartfører	SS-Standartenführer
14	—	SS-nestbrigadefører	SS-Oberführer
15	—	SS-brigadefører	SS-Brigadeführer
—	Stabsjef	Stabsleder	—

PLATE 5.
SS rank collar patches as worn by the Norwegian SS.

PLATE 6
1. Shoulder cord for SS-mann up to and incl. SS-troppfører.
2. Shoulder cord for SS-neststormfører up to and incl. SS-høvedsmann.
3. Shoulder cord for SS-stormbannfører up to and incl. SS-standart-fører.
4. Shoulder cord for SS-nestbrigadefører and above.
5. Collar patches for the Chief of Staff or the Norwegian SS.

PLATE 7
1. Collar patch for all ranks up to and incl. SS-neststandartfører in the Norwegian SS (the emblem is "SS-solhjulet" or SS sun wheel).
2. Badge worn on the upper right sleeve by all ranks in the Norwegian SS. The usual system of different edgings to differentiate men from leaders was not used, but Jonas Lie is known to have worn this badge piped in aluminium thread.
3. N.S. emblem worn on the upper left sleeve by all ranks in the Norwegian SS ("SS-solørn" or SS sun eagle).
4. Armband worn by all ranks in the Norwegian SS.

PLATE 5

44

4

5

6

10

11

12

PLATE 6

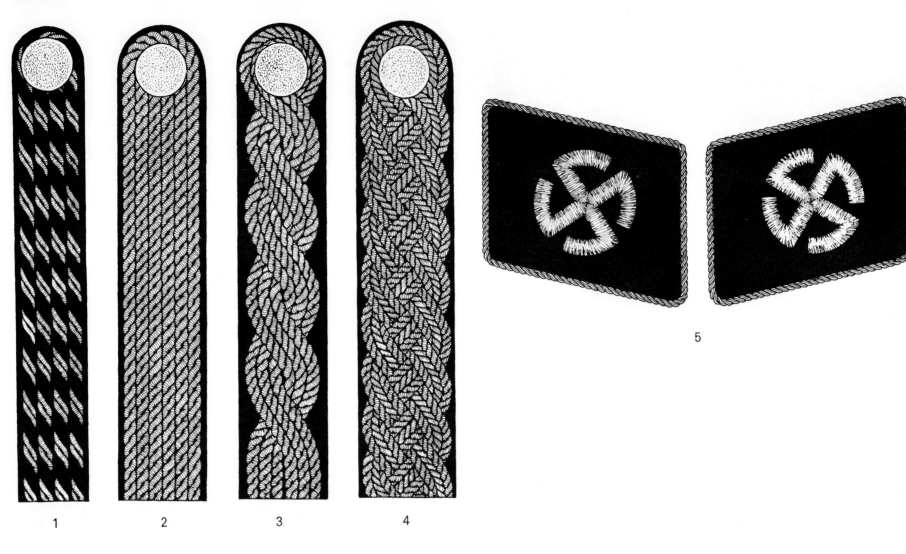

1 2 3 4

5

PLATE 7

1

2

3

4

1. Basic Company flag of the Norwegian SS.

SS FLAGS AND STANDARDS

The Norwegian SS had a number of different patterns of SS flag. Some were printed so that the SS runes were back to front on the reverse. Others were double sided and had either a white or silver fringe. The only official flag, however, was the SS company flag (SS-Stormfane).

2. Named Company flag of the Norwegian SS (here SS-Storm Oslo).

SS STORMFANE
SS Company flag

Black silk flag which measured approximately 100 cms. by 150 cms, in the centre of which were the SS runes in white silk. The flag was edged on three sides with silver fringe. In some cases the company name

OSLO

MIN ÆRE ER TROSKAP

BERGEN

3. Named Company flag of the Norwegian SS with motto (SS-Storm Oslo is the only recorded example of this).

4. Named Company flag of the Norwegian SS.

appeared in silver mock-runic in the top left hand corner, and in others the Norwegian SS motto "Min Ære er Troskap" also appeared under the runes. All recorded flags with company name, or company name plus motto, were not fringed. The pole was made of black polished wood and

was surmounted by a nickel plated lance head, or knob. The overall height of the flag was approximately 3 meters.

The flag was carried by both commissioned and non-commissioned ranks who wore white gloves or gauntlets.

HISTORY OF THE DANISH SS—"SCHALBURG KORPSET"
Motto: Troskab vor Ære

A Nazi party was formed in Denmark in 1929 by Dr. Frits Clausen and was called the D.N.S.A.P. (Denmark's National Socialist Labour Party, "Danmarks National Socialistiske Arbejder Parti"), but it was small and never attracted a great following. In the 1935 elections it gained no seats whatsoever, but in those of 1939 obtained 3. However, Germany invaded Denmark on April 9th, 1940, and it was collaboration under occupation that was to boost membership. 1943 brought an increase in Danish Nazi votes from 31,000 the year before to 43,000. Upon the arrival of the Germans the Danish King and some of his ministers accepted the occupation, and on April 11th a coalition government was formed under Stauning, with the democratic parties in parliament forming a co-operation committee. In July, Erik Scavenius was put in charge of foreign affairs. Scavenius had shown pro-German leanings during the First World War, and on July 8th issued a declaration of collaboration with Germany. In November, Clausen, who had been kept very much in the background, tried a coup which met with complete failure. In early 1941 the Germans tried to have Stauning replaced, but this did not succeed. They did, however, from then on increase their efforts to absorb Denmark into the "New Europe" and promoted Danish-German relations. In July 1941 Danish volunteers formed the "Frikorps Danmark" (Danish Free Corps) to which Scavenius had given his permission, but this led to a crisis and Scavenius threatened to resign.

Stauning died in May 1942 and Vilhelm Buhl took over as Social Democratic prime minister.

From the beginning the Danish people resisted all forms of collaboration. Members of the "Frikorps Danmark" were physically abused and branded as traitors on their return home on leave in September 1942. The Germans' dream of a peaceful occupation faded and matters came to a head in November 1942 when Hitler considered a telegram from the Danish King cold and unfriendly. The Germans seized the opportunity to force an ultimatum and they demanded Buhl's resignation and the establishment of a quisling government. Scavenius accepted the leadership, but with much resentment from people and parliament.

General der Infanterie Hermann von Hanneken was sent to take over command of the German forces of occupation in Denmark and in November, plenipotentary in Denmark, Dr. Werner Best followed, who demanded from the Danish people some 50,000 volunteers for the Eastern Front, an altogether unrealistic figure in view of the country's size and hostile attitude to collaboration. But Best appears to have been fairly intelligent, and he did attempt to curry favour with and obtain support from the Danes. Consequently an election was permitted in March 1943.

There was a large poll, and in fact the D.N.S.A.P. increased its vote and still had three freely elected members in Parliament. Clausen had naturally hoped to do much better and the poor result was not only a great blow to him, it also disenchanted his German masters who lost all interest in him and his party. During mid-1943 German-Danish relations deteriorated and in August riots broke out all over the country accompanied by acts of sabotage. On August 28th, Best handed the government an ultimatum demanding martial law and the death sentence for sabotage and other such acts, which was rejected almost immediately. As a result, the German commander in chief, von Hanneken, took over and proclaimed martial law himself. The Danish armed forces were disbanded on September 28th, 1943, and the comparatively peaceful period of the German occupation of Denmark came to an end.

So until 1943 the Germans carried on a purely military rule and did not interfere seriously with Danish internal affairs. The Danish King and government had formed the main rallying point for the Danish people, and consequently the Danish Nazi party was virtually ignored. Such was the weak standing of Danish Nazism during the first part of the German occupation, and it was because of this weakness that a political SS formation was not established in that country until 1943, and then not as a formation of the D.N.S.A.P.—in fact it had nothing to do with that party whatsoever. As a result the D.N.S.A.P.'s paramilitary formation the Storm Afdelingen ("S.A."—the Danish equivalent of the German S.A.) remained the principal party organization.

Himmler had long considered Denmark ideally suited for a Germanic SS extension to the Allgemeine-SS, but found it much more difficult to establish a branch there than in Holland, Flanders and Norway, for unlike these countries Denmark still retained its King and Government, and both violently objected to the idea. As a result it was not until 1943 that such a formation was established, and so in contrast to the other three branches of the Germanic SS it came not in the early days of occupation as a reward for collaboration, but rather at a much later date and in an atmosphere of acute hostility towards the Germans in general, and the Nazis in particular.

Denmark's branch of the Germanic SS was called the Schalburg Corps (Schalburg-Korps), and being named after a late Danish Nazi and SS hero it was the only one not to include its country's name in its title. Only in Denmark, therefore, was there such a cult of the personality in the naming of a Germanic SS formation, and to understand its background and the significance of this name some space must be devoted to the man von Schalburg himself.

SS-Obersturmbannführer K. B. Martinsen, founder and leader of the Schalburg-Korps.

CHRISTIAN FREDERIK VON SCHALBURG:

Born April 15th, 1906, in Russia of German-Baltic parents he spent his childhood in his family's home in the Ukraine. He joined the Czarist Cadet Corps and was in this Corps when the October Revolution broke out. Fleeing with his parents to Denmark he joined the Danish Army in 1925 and achieved the rank of lieutenant-captain in the Royal Guard (Kaptajn-løjtnant i Den kgl. Livgarde). Von Schalburg was a true National Socialist and firm supporter of Clausen's D.N.S.A.P. and in fact became national youth leader of that organization (Landsungdomsfører i D.N.S.A.P.) in 1938. When the Finnish-Soviet Winter War broke out he joined as a volunteer officer on the Finnish side, though like most of the Scandinavian volunteers he arrived too late and saw only short service before the war ended on March 13th, 1940. Returning to Denmark he is believed to have resumed his duties in the Royal Guard, only to join the 5th SS Armoured Division "Wiking" of the Waffen-SS in September. While von Schalburg was serving in "Wiking" as a staff officer ("01") it was proposed to form a Danish legion to serve alongside the Waffen-SS, and the formation of the Danish Free Corps ("Frikorps Danmark") was first announced on June 28th, 1941, and it was ordered to commence training in Hamburg on July 15th, with the first members leaving Copenhagen on the 19th.

The first commander of the Danish Free Corps was Legion-Obersturmbannführer C. P. Kryssing (formerly a lieutenant-colonel in the Danish Army and commander of the 5th Artillery Battalion), who had volunteered to take command on July 3rd, 1941, although he was in no way a supporter of National Socialism or Clausen's party. Kryssing thought of the Free Corps as having but one purpose, and that was fighting Bolshevism, and he did not consider it part of the National Socialist movement at all. Kryssing's attitude understandably angered Himmler and Berger and the problem came to a climax when a close friend of Kryssing's, Legion-Hauptsturmführer Thor-Jørgensen, was relieved as operations officer of the

Free Corps and sent to SS-Junkerschule "Bad Tölz" (the principal officer training school of the Waffen-SS for 'Germanic' volunteers). Kryssing took this action as a deliberate blow at the leadership of the Free Corps and in retaliation he adopted a policy of passive resistance and allowed the unit's training programme to fall behind. As a result Himmler dismissed Kryssing from his command of the Free Corps on February 8th, 1942, and appointed von Schalburg to take his place shortly afterwards (February or March, 1942). Von Schalburg commanded the Free Corps until June 2nd, 1942, when he was killed near Demjansk leading his men into their first combat engagement. He died holding the rank of an SS-Obersturmbannführer, and as such a fully fledged member of the SS.

After his death, von Schalburg was succeeded as commander of the Frikorps Danmark by Hans-Albert von Lettow-Vorbeck, but the latter was also killed soon after on June 11th. SS-Obersturmbannführer Knud Børge Martinsen then took command, and held this post from June 11th, 1942, until May, 1943. It was Martinsen who, apparently with direct authorisation from Himmler, founded the Danish branch of the Germanic SS on February 2nd, 1943. At first it was called the "Germanic Corps" (Germansk Korps), and in a circular letter dated April 1st, 1943, Martinsen called for its foundation "to strengthen the bonds that bind us together after the struggle on the Eastern Front and to further National Socialist ideas". An appendix to this letter, prepared by Martinsen's deputy, SS-Obersturmführer H. Ellekilde, stated that all young men of "Nordic-Germanic blood" were eligible, provided that they were in good health. It also stated that the Corps had no connection whatsoever with any political parties or groups.

Soon after its foundation, the "Germanic Corps" was renamed, possibly to avoid confusion with the IIIrd (Germanic) SS Armoured Corps (III. (germanisches) SS-Panzer-Korps) that had been founded within the Waffen-SS by an order dated March 30th, 1943. The new name chosen was "Schalburg Corps" (Schalburg-Korps), which honoured the memory of one whom Himmler and the SS almost certainly considered Denmark's best example of an SS officer.

With this change in title, and for other reasons, the exact sequence of events in the early days of the Danish political SS is unclear. February 2nd, 1943, is given as the date of its foundation, yet it was not until July that Martinsen organised the Schalburg Corps during a fortnight's leave at home from the Frikorps Danmark. This delay of some five or six months is hard to understand, unless either Martinsen only formulated the idea of the Corps in February, submitted it, and waited for it to go through channels until July, or he first gathered a cadre together and sent them off for training. The latter explanation appears the more likely, for in the circular letter of April 1st, 1943, six weeks' training courses were prescribed at the Schalburg School (Schalburg-Skolen) and the first of these was from May 1st to June 13th, 1943. With the first course thus ending in mid-June it is understandable how Martinsen organised the Corps in July, but even so the delay of about four months from January 2nd to May 1st is still unexplained.

Whatever the solution, Martinsen did organise the Schalburg Corps in July 1943, and his leave finished, he handed over its command temporarily to his deputy, SS-Obersturmführer H. Ellekilde, until he returned to Denmark in September.

The aim of the Corps was described by Martinsen as being "a prouder, more self-asserting and a stronger Denmark", and he also stated that it was un-political, not intended to interfere with Danish home politics, and in no way seeking for political representation. He said it did, on the other hand, "seek to promote understanding of the Danish race and the value of the Danish Nordic blood, and spread and defend the doctrine of the national folk community". He described its most noble task as "protecting those values of the Danish people that lie anchored within the blood, and at the same time fearlessly defeating all non-Danish and un-nordic influences". Also it set out to "educate the people of the origin of life and the culture in good blood and thereby save the Danish people from the endless un-Nordic sleep".

Membership of the Schalburg-Korps required complete self-sacrifice, in

Christian Frederik von Schalburg, commander of the Frikorps Danmark.

Martinsen's words: "The individual means nothing—our people everything. Our own wishes and aims mean nothing when it concerns the home country. We have to consider no reward—for us all that counts is to sacrifice everything, even life itself, where the homeland is concerned. Our free will shall give way to obedience, we will willingly submit ourselves to the laws of this iron-fisted Corps". And the position of those opposed to the ideals of the Corps was made quite clear from the beginning: "He that sins against our blood does not belong with us; he that does not keep his race holy is not recognized by us; he that breaks his faith with us shall be destroyed".

Apart from their active duties, members of the Schalburg-Korps were also expected to help the Danish volunteers serving with the Waffen-SS, protect their families at home, defend the memory of those that had been killed in action, and carry on the fight for the cause for which they had given their lives. In part fulfilment of these duties a monthly minimum contribution of 2 Kroner was levied upon all members, half of which went to the Schalburg Fund.

Membership of the Corps was restricted to Danes able to bear arms who were of Aryan descent and who submitted themselves to the laws of the Corps. Those that had not fought against Bolshevism on the Eastern Front had first to pass through a six weeks' course at the Schalburg School with satisfactory results. Anyone convicted of a criminal offence was ineligible.

At the time the Schalburg-Korps was founded the situation in Denmark was fast becoming critical, and by September 1943 Danish feeling was so strong against the Nazis that the D.N.S.A.P. was on the point of being dissolved, and it was further aggravated by inner conflict. At this time it was decided to concentrate what Nazi sympathisers there were in Denmark around the Schalburg-Korps, which since its formation had been divided into two distinct groups. Danish SS propaganda described Group I as being the active and uniformed section which could bear arms, and which could only be joined after successfully passing through the Schalburg School or, alternatively, after having served satisfactorily on the Eastern Front. To be eligible one had to be capable of bearing arms, of a Nordic outlook, of a minimum height of 168cms. and fully developed both in body and mind. In effect the real purpose of the Schalburg-Korps' Group I was to serve as a recruiting unit for the Waffen - SS, although later it actually trained Danes for service. The Danish SS definition of the civilian Group II of the Schalburg-Korps was that it "comprised those men who are at the disposal of the Corps but who are prevented from carrying on their work in Group I". The obligations of membership included political support of the Corps and propaganda activities. Group II was replaced in the autumn of 1943 by the "Peoples' League" (Folksværnet), which had been founded officially on September 29th of that year. It was led by a Luftwaffe Captain by the name of Poul Sommer, a Dane who had already collaborated considerably by forming an auxiliary force for the Luftwaffe, known as "Sommer's Guard Corps" or "The Grey Corps"*. The aim of the "Peoples' League" was "to protect the honour of Denmark through active duty against every form of terror and sabotage". It was divided into two distinct and unarmed groups—one "active" with "SS Major" Max Arildskov as its Inspector, and the other "political". In November/December, 1943, Martinsen and

*Possibly formed after his retirement from the Schalburg Corps.

Sommer quarrelled and Allied Intelligence later attributed this to the fact that Martinsen had not been consulted over Sommer's appointment as head of Group II. Evidence was to hand, the intelligence reports state, that a number of charges of fraud were pending against Sommer, and Martinsen objected so violently that he actually went so far as to resign his command of the Schalburg Corps. Sommer then took over command of Group I, but met with such opposition from its members that he was forced to retire and Martinsen was asked to return. The latter agreed to do so only on the condition that Sommer be removed completely from the Corps as a whole, and he further requested that an agreement be drawn up and signed by Dr. Best and the Germanische Leitstelle on the one side and Popp-Madsen and himself on the other, securing the independence of the Corps and preventing interference from the German authorities, who would agree to deal only with Martinsen in person. He succeeded, and this agreement was signed by all parties.

The dismissal of Sommer resulted in the disbandment of the "political" section of the "Peoples' League", and this was replaced by the "Danish Peoples' League" ("Danske Folksværn") under Martinsen, Poul Rasmussen and Popp-Madsen.** The "active" section continued under Arildskov, but on January 9th, 1944, was renamed "Landstormen", with its headquarters in the Freemasons' Lodge (Frimurerlogen) in Copenhagen. Officially the "Landstormen" was an independent organisation, but in fact it took its orders from the Schalburg Corps and can be considered as a part of that Corps. Its aim was to protect the families of the East Front volunteers and it was organised into two sections. The first was the "Skytterkredsen", made up of 500 men who practised shooting in the evenings and during their spare time. The other was a uniformed formation ("Uniformeret Afdeling"), made up of some 200 members.

**One source states that the "Danish Peoples' League" was not a direct offshoot of the Schalburg Corps, but was rather a separate party which voluntarily accepted Martinsen as its leader. It had a "militia" of its own, which it placed at the disposal of the Schalburg Corps.

Memorial service for members of the Danish Free Corps killed in Russia, in Copenhagen on the 17th October, 1943. From l. to r. SS-Obersturmbannführer K. B. Martinsen, SS-Sturmbannführer Boysen, Schalburg's son and widow, and Dr. Werner Best.   (Nationalmuseet.)

Schalburg Corps recruits arriving at the Ringstad Station near Copenhagen accompanied by a Luftwaffe band. (Museet for Danmarks Frihedskamp.)

Meanwhile, other important changes had been made to the organisation of the Schalburg Corps.

One Danish source states that around August, 1943, the majority of the Corps' members were taken into an SS training battalion, named SS-uddannelsesbatallion "Sjælland". War-time Allied Intelligence also reported the existence of this battalion in connection with the Schalburg Corps, but under different names:

(a) Btl. "A", SS-Regiment "Danmark" (which, if reliable, suggests a connection with SS-Grenadier-Regiment "Danmark" of the Waffen-SS Division "Nordland");

(b) SS-Ausbildungs-Btl. "Schalburg".

Other reports exist, however, stating that the latter was not formed until July, 1944, so the exact picture is still unclear.

This battalion contained 300 to 500 men and was commanded at first by SS-Sturmbannführer Poul Neergaard-Jacobsen, and from August 3rd, 1944, by SS-Obersturmführer Egill Poulsen. It had troops in Slagelse, Naestved, Køge and, from February 26th, 1945, Fredericia and Aarhus. The battalion's mission is reported as the protection of crossroads and railways from sabotage.

In the spring of 1944 some members of the Corps, including its intelligence section the E.T., were sent on a three weeks' propaganda tour of Germany, but in fact found themselves on a demolition and sabotage course at Neustrelitz. Upon their return to Denmark several were approached by strangers passing themselves off as members of the Corps who induced them to make careless statements about the Corps. Those that fell for the ruse were arrested and brought before SS-Hauptsturmführer Issel (alias "Waldenburg" and the second chief of SS-Sonderkommando Dänemark), who offered them the choice between front line service in the SS or a term in a concentration camp—they naturally chose the former.

At about the same time (spring 1944) the strength of the Corps was increased to four rifle companies of 120 men each and a guard company. In June, 1944, following the general strike in Copenhagen, the Danish demand for the disbandment of the Schalburg Corps was met by the transfer of all personnel to the Ringsted barracks, not far from the capital. The battalion that had in fact evolved from the Schalburg Corps was officially barracked at Ringsted from July 11th, 1944. At the beginning of 1945 its title was altered to "SS Guard Battalion Seeland" ("SS vagtbatallion Sjælland", or SS-Wach-Btl. Sjælland" in German) and it served during the last months of the war in various acts of sabotage. To the end its commander was Egill Poulsen, who held the title "Btlkdr. und SS-Standortführer".

The Schalburg Corps is reported to have been wound up in January, 1945, and finally disbanded on February 28th, 1945, although as seen above its members continued to serve in a Danish SS battalion. Photographs exist, however, of Corps members being disarmed, either by the Resistance or by British troops, which would indicate that the Corps' uniforms were at least worn until the cessation of hostilities on Danish soil.

In conclusion it may be surmised that although the Schalburg Corps was begun as a branch of the Germanic SS, and as such a Danish equivalent of the German General SS, the fierce Danish hostility to collaboration forced the Corps to be mobilised and concentrated into a full-time security unit. Martinsen himself may well have hoped that the Corps would become a new Danish Army, and this theory is strengthened by the Corps' use of Danish Army uniforms, buttons and cockades, and the Danish coat of arms worn on the sleeve rather than the usual SS symbol of the other Germanic SS formations.

Note: Von Schalburg and the Schalburg Corps have left their mark on the Danish language with the word "schalburgtage", meaning counter-sabotage.

"GERMANISCHE SS DÄNEMARK"

Allied intelligence reports state that the "Germanische SS Dänemark" was founded in October 1944 as a club and welfare organization for former members of the Waffen-SS in Denmark, and it is possible that this is a confusion with the Schalburg-Korps itself. As this term would fit exactly a Germanic SS formation in Denmark—as the Schalburg-Korps undoubtedly was—it may well be that the Schalburg-Korps was finally identified by the title "Germanische SS (in) Dänemark", or its equivalent in Danish. This is borne out by the fact that all officers were of Danish nationality as shown in the organization chart reproduced below:

District I: (Copenhagen, Sjælland, Bornholm)
                SS-Ostuf. Tage Petersen

District II: (Fyn)
                SS-Ustuf. Hartvig Larsen

District III: (North Jutland)
                no 'leiter' appointed

District IV: (Mid Jutland)
                SS-Hstuf. Lorenz Lorenzen—I/C
                SS-Ustuf. Kaare Abraham—2. I/C

District V: (South Jutland)
                SS-Ostuf. Johann Anthon Thorius I/C

District VI: (Bornholm)
                included for all purposes in District I.

The "Germanische SS Dänemark" came under the Germanische Leitstelle.

It may well be that the "Germanische SS Dänemark" was quite separate from the Schalburg-Korps and in fact was an extension of the Waffen-SS, rather than Allgemeine-SS. A point in favour of this supposition is that all the above commanders, although Danish nationals, were Waffen-SS officers and identified by Waffen-SS ranks—not those of the Schalburg-Korps.

OPLÆRING
Training

When the Schalburg Corps was founded on February 2nd, 1943, its address was given as "The Schalburg School, Høvelte near Birkerød" ("Schalburg-Skolen, Høvelte pr. Birkerød") and six weeks' training courses were held there, with the first beginning on May 1st, and ending on June 13th, 1943. This school was commanded by SS-Untersturmführer Søren Kam and its purpose was described as "giving the pupils instruction in the use of weapons and military sports and to provide them with a good knowledge of the Nordic-Germanic 'Weltanschauung' ". In December, 1943, the training of recruits for the Schalburg Corps was moved to Karsemoselejren, near Asserbo in N. Sjælland, and the original school at Høveltegaard was used only to train NCOs (it became known as Underofficersskolen, Høveltegaard, and had a staff of 50 men). In February, 1944, another school was opened at the Ringsted barracks near Copenhagen, and this replaced Korsemose, which was then used as

Probationary members of the Schalburg Corps at training.

a holiday camp for relatives of serving Danish SS men. In June the entire complement of the Corps transferred to Ringsted, and was reorganised as a training battalion.

ORGANISATION

Organization

The Schalburg Corps was originally situated at the Schalburg School at Høvelte (Høveltegaard), near Birkerød. In 1943 its headquarters were moved to the Freemasons' Lodge (Frimurerlogen) at Blegdamsvej 23, København Ø., but are also reported as being at the K.B.-Hall, Peter Bangsvej, København F. In June 1944 it transferred completely to the Ringsted barracks near Copenhagen, and became a training battalion. The following is the organisation of the Schalburg Corps as in November, 1943:

KORPSLEDELSEN
Corps Leadership (Staff)
KORPS-CHEF:
Commander:
    SS-Obersturmbannführer Knud Børge Martinsen
    (10.10.1944-22.1.1945: T.I.P.O. Madsen)
STABSCHEF:
Chief of Staff:
    Kaptajnløjtnant Svend Birkedal-Hansen (for a short time only, as the title of "Chief of Staff" was abolished and replaced by two adjutants—Kaptajn Jacob Holm and SS-Obersturmführer Kund Thorgils)
POLITISK RAADGIVERE:
Political Consultants:
    Dr. jur. Popp-Madsen & Direktør Poul C. Rasmussen
PROPAGANDAAFDELINGENS CHEF:
Head of Propaganda Section:
    Boghandler Arendt Lemvigh-Müller, later cand. polit. Aage Petersen
AFDELING FOR SKOLING OG VERDENSANSKUELSE:
Department for Schooling and Worldly Outlook:
    Cand. mag. Ejnar Vaaben

PERSONALEAFDELING:
Personnel Section:
    Kaptajn Hansen
AFDELING FOR UDDANNELSE OG REGLEMENTER:
Department for Training and Regulations:
    Premierløjtnant Madsen
KOMMANDANT I HOVEDKVARTERET:
H.Q. Commandant:
    Ritmester Johan Starr
CHEF FOR ADMINISTRATION:
Administration Leader:
    Orlogskaptajn Jens Krandrup
AFDELING FOR RACESPORGSMAAL:
Department for Racial Questions:
    Translatør Aage H. Andersen
EFTERRETNINGSTJENESTEN (E.T.):   SS-Untersturmführer
Information Service: Erik Spleth; from March, 1944:
    Erik V. Petersen

GRUPPE 1:

Group 1:

CHEF: SS-Obersturmbannführer
Commander: Knud Børge Martinsen
    3 infantry companies (120 men each)
    1' 'Kanonkompagni' (infantry gun company, equivalent to the I.G.-Kp. of German infantry regiments— "Kanonkompagni" is pre-1940 Danish army usage, every regiment had one)
Underofficersskolen (NCO school) at Høveltegaard (50 men)
Vagtkompagni (guard company) established in September, 1943, with 100 men

GRUPPE II:

Group II:

CHEF:
Commander: Poul Sommer

Landstormen—evolved from the "active" section of Group II and received this title on January 9th, 1944. Its 700 men were organised into two sections: Skyttekredsen—500 men who practised shooting in the evenings and during there spare time—Uniformeret Afdeling—200 uniformed members.

"Landstormen" had sections in Copenhagen Aarhus, Køge, Ringsted and Vordingsborg.

Unlike all other branches of the Germanic SS and the Allgemeine-SS itself in Germany, the Schalburg-Korps because of its small size was not sub-divided into the usual regiments (Standarten), battalions (Sturmbanne), companies (Stürme), platoons (Trupps), squads (Scharen) and files (Rote), and the departure from the usual form of rank titles confirms this point (for they were not based upon the units above, but were similar to Danish Army usage as regards officers' ranks). It was, on the contrary, originally made up of unspecified-size detachments in most towns on the island of Sjælland. As has been seen above, most members of the Corps, Group I went into an SS training battalion, which in early 1945 was renamed SS-Vagt-Btl. "Sjælland".

EFTERRETNINGSTJENESTEN—E.T.
Information Service

The E.T. was an Intelligence Service created in Denmark in the latter part of 1943. It was a plain clothes intelligence organisation believed to have been to the Schalburg Corps what the S.D. (Sicherheitsdienst) was to the SS in Germany*. As with the S.D., its mission was more sinister than the mere collation of intelligence, and through sabotage, assassinations and other excesses it became much feared.

At first the E.T. was not subdivided, but when Erik V. Petersen took over its command in March 1944 after SS-Untersturmführer Erik Spleth it was reorganised into the following three sections:

*Some sources dismiss the E.T.'s subordination to the Schalburg Corps altogether, and say that it existed parallel to, rather than within it. This theory is supported by the fact that members of the E.T. appear to have worn their special collar patches with stylised "E.T." on non-Schalburg Corps uniforms.

SECTION	COMMANDER	PURPOSE
1. Afdeling	Erik V. Petersen	Control of Danish police
2. Afdeling	Egon Ditlev Nielsen (alias "Svend Staal")	Sabotage, assassinations
3. Afdeling	Norreen	Danish military matters

In April, 1944, the E.T. was withdrawn from the Schalburg Corps and placed directly under the Higher SS and Police Leader in Denmark (HSSuPf Dänemark), which post was then held by SS-Gruppenführer und Generalleutnant der Polizei Günter Pancke. Another source states, however, that it came under SS jurisdiction (and this would mean the HSSuPf rather than the Schalburg Corps) on December 1st, 1944.

Upon the dissolution of the Schalburg Corps in early 1945 the E.T. continued to work on as an independent unit. From March until May, 1945, its organisation was as follows:

SECTION	TITLE/(PURPOSE)	COMMANDER
1	Efterretningstjenestens Registratur (E.T.R.)	
2	(a) "Erik V. Petersens Gruppe" (control of Danish police)	Erik V. Petersen
	(b) Kommandocentralen	
3A	(plain clothes street patrols)	Poul Viggo Justesen
3B	(control of literature)	Poul Viggo Justesen
4	"Schiøler-Gruppe" (sabotage)	Ibsen (alias "Schiøler")
5	HIPO (auxiliary police), with: Udrykningschefenes Stab (staff) 1ste Kompagni (1st company) 2det Kompagni (2nd company) Rekrutmandskapet i Høvelte (recruiting team at Høvelte)	Erik V. Petersen, then Martin Johannes Larsen
6	(local police posts throughout the country)	Henry Jørgen Langfritz
7	(technical section)	

8	(radio service)
9A	Efterretningsafdelingen for København (Copenhagen branches of the E.T.)
9B	Efterretningsafdelingen for Provinsen (E.T. branches for the provinces)
9C	"Jørgen Lorentzen-Gruppen" (Danish resistance)

Of the above sections, 1, 5 and 6 were grouped into the "First Inspectorate" ("1ste Inspektorat") under Norreen, and 3, 7, 8 and 9A-9C into the "Second Inspectorate" ("2det Inspektorat") under Mortensen.

SCHALBURG-FONDEN
The Schalburg Fund

A fund for the Schalburg-Korps ("Schalburg-Fonden") existed from the establishment of the Corps and was at Falkonérgaardsvej 11. Members of the Corps had to make a monthly contribution of at least 2 Kroner, half of which went to the Fund. It was for this reason that no institute for aiding members existed in Denmark as in the other three countries with a Germanic SS, although the strong Danish resentment towards the SS may have been a strong determining factor in this.

Assistance for members of the Corps and the relatives of those that had been killed was channelled exclusively through this Fund, and female relations of members were expected to be at the Corps' disposal for relief work through the Schalburg Fund.

THE BLACK SS SERVICE UNIFORM

The Schalburg-Korps did not wear a provisional uniform, but were issued with the black one at the beginning. It was of German manufacture and will only be described insofar as it differed from the German General SS uniform.

SS VÅBENFRAKKE
SS Service tunic
As German.

SS RIDEBUKSER
SS Breeches
As German.

SS OVERFRAKKE
SS Service overcoat
As German.

SS UNIFORMSHUE
SS Service peaked cap
As German but worn with the Schalburg-Korps emblem in woven silk manufacture in place of the SS emblem (Hoheitsabzeichen). Probationary members appear to have worn neither.

SS STÅLHJELM
SS Steel helmet
Model 1935 German steel helmet sprayed black and with the circular swastika on the right hand side.

SS FODTØJ
SS Footwear
Black leather marching boots
Black leather lace-up ankle boots

SS HANDSKER
SS Gloves
Black leather.
Black wool.
White cloth.

SS UNDERTØJ
SS Underwear
Brown shirt.
White shirt.
Black tie.

SS LÆDERTØJ
SS Leatherware
Black leather belt and cross strap. Other ranks had a special belt buckle, while leaders are thought to have worn the German SS Leaders' belt buckle.

THE MODEL 1923 DANISH KHAKI SERVICE UNIFORM

As the General SS in Germany had in some cases changed over to field grey at the beginning of the war, so the Schalburg Corps was issued with a more practical khaki uniform.

In fact they took over stocks of the 1923 pattern Danish army uniform from the Royal Life Guards on August 29th, 1943. This consisted of tunic and breeches in khaki cloth. The tunics had the original "turned-down" collar altered to a "stand and fall" style, and could be worn either open or closed by officers, but only closed by other ranks. The tunics had two pleated breast pockets and two side pockets. Other ranks wore their trousers (which had turn-ups) rolled up over their black leather lace-up boots, while officers wore either long trousers and black shoes or breeches and boots. All ranks had a double breasted overcoat of Danish origin.

The same basic insignia was worn on the khaki uniform as on the black one, except that Waffen-SS rank insignia replaced the General SS pattern. White piping was used throughout, and so other ranks' shoulder straps should have been in black cloth with white piping. In fact variations to this rule were often worn, such as the khaki Danish shoulder straps with their original narrow green piping, or with the latter replaced by the German white piping.

NCOs wore braid ("Tresse") around their collars and shoulder straps, and the appointment equivalent to the German "SS-Stabsscharführer" wore the double "Tresse" rings around both cuffs.

The grades of other ranks were shown in the Waffen-SS manner by chevrons or a star worn below the national shield on the left sleeve.

Danish army buttons with the three lions passant and nine hearts were worn either in dull gold finish or painted khaki.

The Danish army field cap was worn, with its white and red cockade and Danish braid edge for officers, as well as a khaki peaked cap similar in design to the German mountain or ski cap, but with two Danish buttons on the front and the Danish cockade. The Model 1935 German steel helmet painted khaki and with the circular swastika on the right hand side, was also worn.

Leather equipment was Danish and black for all ranks.

Rifles issued to the Schalburg Corps included the Danish pattern of 1889, the 8mm Krag-Jørgensen Model 1910 with bayonet, and the standard German 98 K carbine. Bergmann sub-machine guns were also used.

SS ARBEJDSUNIFORM
SS Fatigue uniform

While on field training and fatigues members of the Schalburg-Korps wore a light coloured cotton drill uniform. Photographs show this fatigue uniform as having been worn without insignia, but an example has been reported of denims with black Waffen-SS shoulder straps piped in white, Danish army buttons, the national shield with lions and hearts on the left upper sleeve, and possibly an armband.

SS DISTINKTIONER
SS Badges of rank

No rank charts have come to light for the Schalburg-Korps, but photographs suggest that the same badges of rank were worn as in the German SS. In common with the other branches of the Germanic SS, the system of rank insignia adopted on the black uniform was that of the German General SS, but Waffen-SS rank insignia seems to have been worn on the khaki uniform at all times.

SS KRAVEDISTINKTIONER
SS Collar patches

Rank was shown on the left collar patch in the usual way, but as with the Norwegian SS, all members of the Schalburg Corps (with the exception of the E.T.) wore a circular swastika* on the right patch. The two Scandinavian branches of the Germanic SS, therefore, differed from their

*The design of the circular swastika as worn by the Schalburg Corps differed in detail from that of the Norwegian SS (cf. illustrations on pp. 46/47 and 68). The Norwegian "sun wheel" was placed diagonally, whereas that of the Schalburg Corps was placed in an upright position, both in relation to the parallelogram formed by the sides of the collar patch.

Guard outside the Schalburg Corps headquarters at the Freemasons' Lodge in Copenhagen, 1943.

Schalburg Corps men in Danish khaki uniforms stand guard outside their headquarters.

Lowland counterparts in not wearing regimental numerals on the right collar patch, but then this is not surprising as they were not organised in regiments.

It is presumed that any officers with the rank of colonel (Oberst) and above wore their badges of rank on both collar patches, that is if there were any officers of such rank.

SS GRADER
SS Ranks

The following is a comparison chart between the ranks of the Schalburg-Korps and the German General SS :

No.	SCHALBURG-KORPS	ALLGEMEINE-SS
1	Schalburgmand	SS-Mann
2	Tropsfører	SS-Rottenführer
3	Overtropsfører	SS-Unterscharführer
4	Vagtmester	SS-Scharführer
5	Overvagtmester	SS-Oberscharführer
6	Stabsvagtmester	SS-Hauptscharführer
—	—	SS-Stabsscharführer*
7	Fændrik	SS-Sturmscharführer
8	Løjtnant	SS-Untersturmführer
9	Overløjtnant**	SS-Obersturmführer
10	Kaptajn	SS-Hauptsturmführer
11	Major	SS-Sturmbannführer
12	Oberstløjnant	SS-Obersturmbannführer
13	Oberst	SS-Standartenführer

*An appointment, not a rank, but included here as an equivalent did exist in the Schalburg Corps.

**There is no such rank as an Overløjtnant in Denmark, and this is believed to have been a Germanised form of Kaptajnløjtnant.

SCHALBURGKORS
Schalburg Cross

Little is known about this cross, which was named after von Schalburg, and is therefore believed to have been founded for award to members of the Schalburg Corps.

If ever there was a foundation order it has so far not come to light, and according to a former member of the Schalburg Corps the cross was only awarded once, and then to a member of the Corps killed in a skirmish with the Danish resistance movement. Soon after this one and

The Schalburg Cross.   Mollo Collection

only award, the report goes, the Corps' headquarters were set alight by the resistance, and whole boxes of the crosses were either melted down, or strewn over the streets of Copenhagen. Some of these were undoubtedly picked up by passers-by and have since fallen into the hands of collectors.

Unidentified Schalburg Corps leader wearing a Danish tunic.

Unidentified Schalburg Corps man wearing black service dress.

PLATE 8

1. Collar patch presumed to have been worn by all ranks in the Schalburg Corps.
2. Badge worn on the upper left sleeve by all ranks in the Schalburg Corps (in woven silk with blue lions and red hearts on a golden yellow field). Photographs suggest that this badge may also have been manufactured in white metal, although all surviving examples are in cloth.
3. Collar patch for members of the intelligence service of the Schalburg Corps (which appears not to have been worn on the Schalburg Corps' uniform).
4. Armband worn by the Staff, NCO School, Guard Company and Landstormen of the Schalburg Corps (and which was possibly withdrawn when the battalion on Seeland dropped the name "Schalburg").

RIGHT

1. Armband worn by the "Skjalm Hvide" company of the Schalburg Corps (named after the founder of the Hvide dynasty, died 1192).
2. Armband worn by the "Absalon" company of the Schalburg Corps (named after the archbishop who founded Copenhagen, 1128-1201).
3. Armband worn by the "Herluf Trolle" company of the Schalburg Corps (named after the naval hero, 1516-1565).
4. Armband worn by the "Olaf Rye" company of the Schalburg Corps (named after the Norwegian-Danish major-general, 1791-1849).
5. Armband worn by the "Læssøe" company of the Schalburg Corps (named after the lieutenant-colonel, 1811-1850).

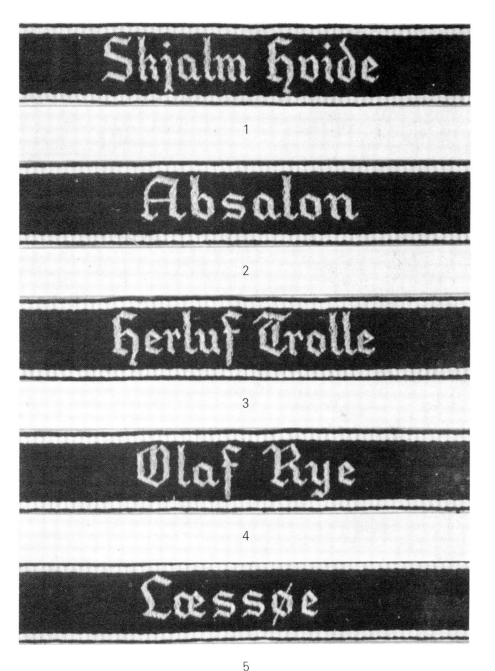

PLATE 8

1

2

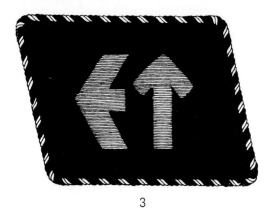

3

Schalburg

4

Flag of the Schalburg Corps. (See caption Plate 8/2, p. 67.)

GERMANISCHE STURMBANNE
Germanic Battalions

In addition to the true Germanic SS, which as has been seen above consisted of political non-German formations in the Germanic countries, special units within the General SS (Allgemeine-SS) were created for Germanic workers in Germany. These units were known as Germanic Battalions (Germanische Sturmbanne), and were open not only to Dutchmen, Flemings, Norwegians and Danes, who had their own Germanic SS formations at home, but also to the Swiss, who did not.

The Germanic Battalions were represented throughout Germany by Special Staffs (Sonderstäbe) attached to those SS Districts containing a high concentration of Germanic labour, and these Special Staffs in turn on occasion maintained Outstations (Aussenstellen). Only 7 out of a total of 24 SS Districts have so far been found to have contained Special Staffs (See Volume 1, page 30).

The Germanic Battalions, their special staffs and outstations were controlled by Section DII la (Abteilung DII 1a) of the SS Main Office, which was titled "The Germanic SS in the Reich" ("Germanische-SS im Reich"). The Section Leader was SS-Untersturmführer (SS-Ustuf. d.R. in the Waffen-SS) Johannes Gustke, and Section Heads (Referenten) looked after the affairs of the Germanic Battalions from Flanders, Holland, Switzerland and Denmark—why there was none for Norway is not known. As well as control from the SS Main Office in Berlin, the Germanic Battalions were subordinate to the local General SS District, and so were therefore special units of the General SS, in theory the Germanic SS in Germany, but in fact recruiting depots for the Waffen-SS. On September 20th, 1942, the newspaper for Dutch workers in Germany, ("Van Honk") stated that its readers could join the "Germanische SS Stormban" (sic), along with Flemings, Danes and Norwegians. The article continued by stating that members would serve in after-work hours and that their duties would include "training and sports" —it was not necessary that they should have belonged to their native Nazi parties, ostensibly on the grounds that the SS was "unpolitical", but in fact because of the bitter opposition between the Nazi parties in the Germanic countries and the SS.

In 1943 Staffs were established of Dutchmen, Flemings and Germans (who, acting as "hosts", provided the cadre), although Danes and Norwegians were also involved at that time. In late 1943, when a Swiss Germanic SS was being planned, provision for the Swiss was made in the Germanic Battalions, and Swiss nationals living in Germany who wished to join the Germanic SS were invited to join "Swiss Battalions" ("Schweizer Sturmbanne"). By December 1st, 1944, a Section Head for the Swiss was in existence in Section DII 1a of the SS Main Office. The strength of the Germanic Battalions was constantly being tapped by the Waffen-SS, particularly for training at the SS camp Sennheim in Alsace. By March 3rd, 1944, the Germanic Battalions contained 2,179 men from Holland, Flanders, Norway, Denmark and Switzerland, and were organized into seven Special Staffs as below:

Spree	(3)	der Germanische SS Sturmbanne Rüdersdorf b. Berlin, Luisenstrasse 44	Ostuf. Barth
Elbe *	(4)	der Germanische SS Sturmbanne Dresden AI, Devrientstrasse 2	Ustuf. Starke
Südwest	(5)	der Germanische SS Sturmbanne Stuttgart, Hegelstrasse 1	Ostuf. Allwicker
West	(6)	der Germanische SS Sturmbanne Düsseldorf, Verdingerstrasse 28	Ustuf. Lüttgen
Nordsee	(10)	der Germanische SS Sturmbanne Hamburg-Altona, Palmaille 59	Scharf. Djuren
Mitte	(11)	der Germanische SS Sturmbanne Braunschweig, Friedr.-Wilhelm-strasse 37	Ostuf. Barren-scheen
Main	(13)	der Germanische SS Sturmbanne Nürnberg, Tufelhofstrasse 26 II	Hstuf. Sievert

*With an Outstation Danube (Aussenstelle Donau) at Fuhrmanngasse 18a, Vienna VIII.

Of the above, Special Staff Nordsee was reported to have absorbed the majority of Flemings, along with a number of Danes and Dutchmen.

A cultural centre for the Germanic SS in Germany was established first in Hannover under the name "Germanische Haus", but it is believed to have been evacuated towards the end of the war to Hildesheim, where it was set up under the name "Haus Germanien". This building also housed the Political Leadership School of the Germanic SS which was commanded by SS-Sturmbannführer (F) Dr Peter Paulsen. A similar "house" was established for the Swiss by Amtsgruppe DI/3 of the SS Main Office in Stuttgart under the name "Panorama-Heim".

"UNIFORMS"

The SS was not slow to appreciate the manpower potential of the "germanic" workers in the Reich, and tried to establish a contact with them at an early stage. The most obvious method of infiltration used and, perhaps, the most pertinent to this book, was the issue of special clothing. When a foreign worker applied for a new issue of working clothes he was given a uniform-like outfit, usually consisting of long black trousers with either boots or shoes, and a khaki-coloured shirt. The SS supplied these "uniforms", but only indirectly as they handed them over to the camp authorities for eventual issue to the workers (in cases of insufficient supply issue depended upon individual need or position on a roster). In spite of this indirect line of supply the SS emphasised to the workers that it was only through their great kindness that such clothes were available, and also made the point that such issue was quite indiscriminate—workers got the clothing if they were members of pro-Nazi organisations or not.

Before the arrival on the scene of the Germanic Battalions, therefore, "germanic" workers in Germany were wearing a sort of uniform, provided by the SS. Those that later joined the Germanic Battalions officially wore no uniforms, except at such times as they attended courses at SS training camps, such as Sennheim, when some at least are known to have been issued with the normal field-grey uniform of the Waffen-SS.

A theory exists, however, based on rather thin photographic evidence, that the Germanic Battalions wore the uniforms and insignia of their native Germanic SS formations. Some take this argument further and suggest that the arm bands worn in Germany carried German translations of those worn by the Germanic SS at home, and examples are said to exist (e.g. "SS-Flandern" instead of "SS-Vlaanderen"). These reports should be treated with caution until proved accurate.

GERMANISCHE STURMBANN DÄNEMARK
Germanic Battalion Denmark

In spite of a lack of information on the Germanic Battalions in general, sufficient material has come to light to make a separate study of the Danish Germanic Battalion worth while.

The Germanic Battalion Denmark (Germanische Sturmbann Dänemark, or G.S.D.) consisted of workers who were employed in Germany with a view to later admission into the SS, and was founded on Danish initiative. Like the Germanic SS it was based on "pan-germanic" thinking, and was not only completely separate from Frits Clausen's small Danish Nazi Party (D.N.S.A.P.) but also totally opposed to it.

While exact dates are not recorded, the G.S.D. is believed to have been begun in Hamburg in early 1942. Substantial interest was aroused among the Danish workers in the north German port and so the authorities experimented in other German towns having large numbers of Danish workers. Thus the organisation spread with groups in many important towns throughout the Reich, and the Berlin group was established in March/April, 1942. The fact that the G.S.D. was given offices in a wing of the SS Main Office at Hagenstrasse 40 (or 45?), Berlin-Grünewald, removes any doubt that the organisation was run and financed by the SS. Once the Germanic Battalion had been established from the Danish workers in Germany there still remained the problem of attracting those still flowing into the Reich. In the case of Berlin there was always at least one representative of the G.S.D. at the railway station to greet a transport of Danish workers, and he would tell them to contact him if they had any problems or needed any help. The next step was to have G.S.D. agents visit the workers in their camps, but on the first visit all they asked was what kind of sports the men were interested in. At this early stage in the programme no mention at all was made of the SS, National Socialism, or even politics in general.

These helpful greetings on arrival and visits to the work camps gave the impression that the G.S.D. was some sort of welfare organisation, and in the light of this the Danish workers were asked to join. Membership required attending lectures on "pan-germanism" and allied subjects, but carried with it the advantage of being able to use sports facilities, which were forbidden to non-members. No pressure was used at this stage to induce members to join any Nazi or associated organisations, but members were urged to participate in various semi-military activities.

The next step was for the G.S.D. to arrange a visit to SS-Ausbildungslager Sennheim in Alsace, on the understanding that the workers who went would attend a course on "pan-germanism", social conditions, and so on. When the G.S.D. members arrived at Sennheim they found matters very different, and their first protest was against the forced issue of SS uniforms, which move was contrary to promises they had received in Berlin. Living conditions at Sennheim were apparently tolerable, but rather than studying subjects as outlined in Berlin, they were put through a 4 to 6 weeks' intensive military training course, which included anti-communist propaganda.

Throughout their stay at Sennheim the G.S.D. members were urged to volunteer for service in the SS on the eastern front, but this campaign proved unsuccessful and no more than 3% actually went into the Waffen-SS.

Once the training course at Sennheim was completed, the G.S.D. members were sent on a fourteen day leave to Denmark, on the strict understanding that they wore their new SS uniforms. Their leave over, they returned to their original working places and apparently had to hand in their SS uniforms, for thenceforth they were forbidden to wear them.

The above information relates to the methods used in Berlin first to draw Danish workers into the G.S.D., and then into the ranks of the Waffen-SS. It is assumed that similar methods were used elsewhere, and were not restricted to the Danish Germanic Battalion.

Frits Clausen, the Danish Nazi leader, was a bitter opponent of the G.S.D., and he urged the Germans to dissolve the organisation. This they did in January 1943, although in fact it was re-established some months later in close collaboration with Clausen and his D.N.S.A.P.

The G.S.D. as such had no special uniforms, insignia, or even membership cards. The SS uniforms they wore while at Sennheim and on leave thereafter are assumed to have been normal Waffen-SS issue.

GERMANISCHE LEISTUNGSRUNE
The Germanic Proficiency Runes

Originally no proficiency badges were available for all branches of the Germanic SS, and in fact only in Holland had any SS sports badges been introduced at all. Himmler, however, wanted a badge that would be available to both the General SS in Germany and the Germanic SS abroad, and which would not only require a high standard in various sports, but also ability in military activities and National Socialist ideology. His reasons for introducing such a badge were many. He wished to encourage his political SS men to keep athletically fit and have their minds well tuned to the Nazi way of thinking, and also to inject into essentially non-combattant SS members a competitive interest in basic military training. On a much grander scale he aimed at strengthening the pan-Germanic idea within the entire political SS organization.

The badge that Himmler introduced was called the Germanic Proficiency Runes (Germanische Leistungsrune), and its very design was geared to appeal particularly to the Germanic SS. For the two victory runes of the SS were superimposed upon a mobile swastika (45 mm. in diameter), the formation sign of the "Wiking" division of the Waffen-SS (later adopted by the entire III. Germanic SS Panzer Corps), which was made up largely of volunteers from the Germanic countries. The badge was instituted in two grades, bronze and silver, with a higher standard required for the attainment of the silver. It was worn in the centre of the left breast pocket of the service uniform.

Once Himmler had decided upon instituting the Germanic Proficiency Runes, he handed over to Berger and his SS-Hauptamt the task of devising the badge's attainment rules and regulations. These were published on July 15th, 1943, and the introduction ran as follows:

"Regulations for the Award of the Germanic Proficiency Runes

The Germanic Proficiency Runes shall be awarded to those that have distinguished themselves in sports competitions and shown spiritual

The Germanic Proficiency Runes in bronze. Mollo collection.

maturity and sound personal thinking in the ideological field. It can be won by German and other Germanic men.

To be qualified for the Germanic Proficiency Runes one must fulfil the regulations laid down in the following three categories:

(1) Individual achievement;

(2) Team achievement;

(3) Tests in theoretical education (ideology).

The award shall be made by the Chief of the SS-Hauptamt following

consultation with the Reichsführer-SS. Recipients of the Germanic Proficiency Runes receive at the same time a diploma witnessing the award.

Those that wish to try for the Germanic Proficiency Runes and are not members of the Germanic SS, nor aspirants in that organization, must hold a political leaders' card issued by an SS service centre to be able to join a preparation course. The test for the Germanic Proficiency Runes requires a preparation of three weeks. Applicants must then take part in a course laid down for the attainment of the Proficiency Runes, or be able to complete 120 satisfactory hours of training, which must not be spread over more than six consecutive months.

The test shall be carried out by a fully qualified representative of the SS-Hauptamt, Instruction Section, assisted by two members of a Germanic SS service centre. The Proficiency Runes shall be worn on the left side of the uniform, more correctly with service dress.

The Chief of the SS-Hauptamt can from time to time insist that the tests be taken again. Those unable to achieve the requirements, or who do not take part, forfeit the badge.

It is at the discretion of the Chief of the SS-Hauptamt whether or not the badge shall be withdrawn on account of minor infringements or for other reasons.

Berlin, July 15th, 1943.
Reichsführer-SS
Chief of SS-Hauptamt
(signed) Berger."

From his field headquarters on August 15th, 1943, Himmler officially introduced the Germanic Proficiency Runes. In the institution document he stated that it "should be an example in physical training and tests in the use of weapons in the National Socialist spirit, and confirmation of the voluntary attainment of the Germanic joint destiny". His introduction ended by referring to the rules and regulations for the attainment of the badge that had been prepared by the SS-Hauptamt, and which are reproduced in full on page 75.

The first award ceremony of the Germanic Proficiency Runes held at the Dutch SS School Avegoor on February 1st, 1944. From left to right: SS-Obergruppenführer Berger (Chief of SS-Hauptamt), Reichsführer-SS Heinrich Himmler, Dr. Seyss-Inquart (Reichskommissar in Holland), Mussert (leader of the N.S.B.), and Feldmeijer (Voorman of the Dutch SS).

Stiftungsurkunde

In großer Zeit, in der über die Zukunft Europas entschieden wird und germanische Freiwillige sich in der Waffen-SS an der Seite des deutschen Soldaten im Kampfe bewähren, stifte ich die

Germanische Leistungsrune.

Sie soll sein

ein Ansporn für Leibesertüchtigung und Wehrerziehung im Geiste der nationalsozialistischen Weltanschauung und eine Bestätigung des freiwilligen Bekenntnisses zur germanischen Schicksalsgemeinschaft

und wird in zwei Leistungsstufen verliehen.

Ich genehmige hiermit die mir vom Chef des SS-Hauptamtes vorgelegten Bestimmungen für die Verleihung der Leistungsrune und die Prüfungsbedingungen.

Feldkommandostelle, den 15. August 1943.

H. Himmler.

The institution document for the Germanic Proficiency Runes signed by Himmler

---

Requirements for the Award of the Germanic Proficiency Runes
GROUP I: INDIVIDUAL PERFORMANCE

(Each test to be judged separately).

A: PHYSICAL TESTS

		MINIMUM REQUIREMENTS		
No.	TEST	BRONZE	SILVER	DRESS
1.	400 meter sprint	$72\frac{1}{2}$ secs.	68 secs.	Sports kit
2.	Long jump	4 meters	$4\frac{3}{4}$ meters	,,
3.	Grenade throw	35 meters	45 meters	,,

Tests 1-3 must be carried out during a single day

4. Choice of exercises: *   *   ,,
riding, motor sport, winter sports, etc.

* To pass this unspecified test satisfactorily, the applicant must fulfil the conditions required for the award of the National Sports Badge ("Reichssportabzeichen"), or receive a certificate for solo flying, or pass with distinction in riding, motor sport, winter sports, etc.

5. Swimming 300 meters   12 mins.   9 mins.   Sports kit
Tests 1-5 to be performed following normal competition rules.

B: DEFENCE SPORTS

6. Free hand shooting with   40 points   60 points   Service small caliber, 10 shots prone,   uniform 50 meters from target.
2 test shots allowed which are shown separately. Shooting on a new instruction target for each shot. Time limit of 10 minutes— shots fired after time is up invalidate the test.

7. Field Exercises: Service
   (a) Description of a terrain;   Good   Excellent   uniform judgment of a terrain for a particular purpose e.g. approach possibilities.

7. (b) Estimation of 3 distances (near, intermediate, far); estimation of 2 distances sideways.

    3 satisfactory estimates (margin of error allowed 30%)

    (c) Orientation following points in the terrain; knowledge of the elementary rules in the use of map and compass.   Good   Excellent

    (d) Description of terrain and passing on of information (moving up in a terrain that can be observed by the enemy).   Good   Excellent

    (e) Camouflage against detection by the enemy according to the principle of "See and not be seen"; observation and description of objective.   Good   Excellent

Tests 6 and 7 : carried out during a temporary stay or training period in the respective SS school. The men are tested one at a time on selected positions of the terrain.

Test 7 (a) to (e) may be omitted by candidates that have completed six months military service.

GROUP II : TEAM PERFORMANCE

On the basis of individual performance the training leaders (invigilators) select teams of 4 to 6 men.

A : PHYSICAL TESTS

8. 100 meter relay   17 secs.   14½ secs. Sports kit
9. Rope climbing   12 secs.   9 secs.   ,,

Test 9 : Conflicting versions have been found, and both will be given :

Norwegian : Each team has two 5 meter long ropes that hang free, 80 cms. apart. Each man climbs the first rope, changes over to the other, and lowers himself down on it.

Dutch : Each team has to climb three 5 meter long ropes which are suspended from a carrying frame 60 cms. apart. The men have to climb up one rope, touch the carrying frame, and then descend by the other.

Mutual assistance was permitted in Test 9.

10. 110 meter obstacle race with grenade throw.   60 secs. 50 secs. Service uniform

Obstacles : Canal : 3 meters long, 1 meter deep.
          Wall : 2 meters high.
          Crawling obstacle : 0.50 meters high, 4 meters long.
          Climbing obstacle : (cross beams) 0.90 meters high.
          Defence trenches : on the 110 meter finishing line.

Throwing target : a crater 5 meters in diameter the centre of which is 20 meters from the finishing line.

Width of path and obstacles : 4 meters.

Time calculation is to allow for throwing the hand-grenades. The men start in closed formation equipped with 3 grenades each, and mutual assistance is permitted. The grenades are to be thrown from cover, and the men are permitted to get up on their knees for a moment to throw the grenades. The race finishes as soon as the last participant is standing upright in the shelter having throw his last grenade.

11. 2,000 meter cross-country   10 mins.   8 mins.   Service
                                                       uniform

Each team has to cover a distance of 2,000 meters in closed formation in as short a time as possible. Mutual assistance may be given.

12. 30 kilometer march with $9\frac{1}{2}$ hours $9\frac{1}{2}$ hours   Service
obstacles   uniform

The march is divided as follows: $\frac{3}{4}$ along paths; $\frac{1}{4}$ across terrain.

Programme: (1) Departure 3 hours before sunrise; night march of about 15 kilometers;

(2) Putting up camp with tents, constructing cooking facilities; technical skills; training breaking up camp; 3 hours allowed which must be carefully observed.

(3) return march including overcoming terrain obstacles. The last 5 kilometers of the march to be in closed formation.

(4) March equipment.

GROUP III: PHILOSOPHY

13. Written (choice of subject). Time Limit: Good   Excellent
2 hours. At the Dutch SS school Avegoor the choice of subjects was as follows: (1) "Our enemies";

(2) "Being a Germanic and becoming one";

(3) "People and fatherland".

14. Oral group discussion on the National   Good   Excellent
Socialist theme. Test covers the same subjects as Test 13.

If the candidate does not comply with the conditions as laid down above, he may re-apply for the Germanic Proficiency Runes in six months' time after further training.

The Germanic Proficiency Runes were open to members of the German General SS, but to keep within the framework of this book only the awards to Germanic SS personnel will be described. Although all four branches of the Germanic SS were eligible and the rules and requirements were published in the newspapers of each, record has only been found of awards in Holland, Denmark and Norway. It is possible that the Runes were awarded to members of the Flemish SS, but as this formation was on the decline in 1944 it is believed that none of its members received them.

Only one presentation ceremony is recorded for each of the three countries concerned, although there may have been others later in the war. The awards in Holland, Denmark and Norway are described in detail below, and the names given to the Germanic Proficiency Runes in these countries are also listed.

Holland:
Germaansche Leistungsrune

The first awards of the Germanic Proficiency Runes were made by Himmler when he visited the Dutch SS School Avegoor, near Arnheim, on February 1st, 1944. He was greeted by the Higher SS and Police Leader in Holland, SS-Obergruppenführer Rauter, and also present at the ceremony were Reichskommissar Seyss-Inquart, leader of the N.S.B. Mussert, and Chief of the SS-Hauptamt, SS-Obergruppenführer und General der Waffen-SS Berger.

Several thousand had applied for the badge and undergone the tests, but only 95 had passed, and these are reported as having been made up of SS leaders, political leaders, Dutch and German SS men, and Dutch and German policemen. Photographs of the ceremony suggest that members of the Dutch SS were in the majority.

Himmler presented the badges personally, taking them from a board carried by an Unterscharführer from the "Germania" regiment of the "Wiking" SS division, and made a speech praising the achievements of the Dutch SS (and the "Westland" regiment in particular), and upgraded the Dutch Volunteer Legion to a grenadier brigade (SS-Grenadier-brigade "Nederland").

Denmark:

SS-Æresruner
SS-Ærestegn

The only recorded awards of the Germanic Proficiency Runes in Denmark were made at Høvelte on June 2nd, 1944, by the Chief of the SS-Hauptamt, SS-Obergruppenführer und General der Waffen-SS Berger. The presentation was made at a memorial ceremony for SS volunteers from Denmark killed in action, and in fact the test schedule had been timed so that the results would be ready for this ceremony.

Berger spoke of the Danish SS volunteers killed in action, and how "their spirits could rest in peace knowing that new columns of Germanic fighters stood behind them." He stated that it was in the memory of the dead Danish SS volunteers and in their spirit that the first Germanic Proficiency Runes were being awarded on Danish soil.

No details are available of the number of badges actually awarded, nor of the recipients. However, photographs suggest that the badges went to members of the Schalburg Corps, who were wearing the black service uniform.

SS-Hoofdstormleider Bettink wearing the Leistungsrune and Feldmeijer in field-grey uniform.

Norway:
Germanske Runemerke
Germanske Dugleiksrune

The only recorded awards of the Germanic Proficiency Runes in Norway were made at the Norwegian SS School on August 16th, 1944, when the Higher SS and Police Leader in Norway, SS-Obergruppenführer Rediess, acting upon instructions from Himmler, awarded ten in silver and fifteen in bronze to members of the Norwegian SS. Also present at the ceremony were SS-neststandartfører Riisnæs, and the leader of the Germanische Leitstelle in Norway, SS-Sturmbannführer Leib.

Once the commander of the Norwegian SS School had bade his guests welcome, Rediess spoke of the badge's meaning, and how the 25 recipients had, though their behaviour, been a good example to their comrades in the Germanic SS, and to the youth of Norway. He then presented the 25 badges to the Norwegian SS men.

After the awards SS-neststandartfører Riisnæs made a short speech on the meaning of the victory runes of the SS and the sun-wheel (which two emblems made up the design of the Rune Badge), as well as of the swastika. He ended by stressing the need for volunteers for the front lines, in his words, "to enable the SS to achieve the final victory".

SS-mann of the Norwegian SS wearing the Germanic Proficiency Runes.

BIBLIOGRAPHY

(a) General

Egon Alois Bartetzko, Thesis on MILITARY COLLABORATION IN THE GERMANIC COUNTRIES, University of California, 1966.

Dr. K.-G. Klietmann, DIE WAFFEN-SS, Verlag "Der Freiwillige", Osnabrück, 1965.

David Littlejohn, M.A., A.L.A., and Col. C. M. Dodkins, D.S.O., O.B.E., ORDERS, DECORATIONS, MEDALS AND BADGES OF THE THIRD REICH (INCLUDING THE FREE CITY OF DANZIG), R. James Bender Publishing, California, 1968.

George H. Stein, THE WAFFEN-SS, Cornell University Press, New York, 1966.

STELLENBESETZUNG DES SS-HAUPTAMTES—STAND 1.12.1944.

(b) Holland

DOCUMENTATIE—information booklet for use in the collaboration trials, produced immediately after the war.

FOTONIEUWS, DE SPIEGEL DER BEWEGING—monthly illustrated magazine.

GERMANISCHE REIHE, Niederländische Ausgabe den Haag—Dutch edition of the German SS monthly.

HAMER, MAANDBLAD VAN DE VOLKSCHE (later GERMAANSCHE) WERKGEMEENSCHAP—monthly magazine.

NATIONAAL-SOCIALISTISCH JAARBOEK 1942.

NATIONAAL-SOCIALISTISCHE ALMANAK 1943 & 1944.

Organisatieleider der N.S.B., DISTINCTIEVEN DER BEWEGING.

DE RIJKS GEDACHTE 1940/1943, Storm, Amsterdam, 1944.

SS-LEITHEFT VOOR NEDERLAND—monthly magazine started in January 1944 and continued into 1945.

SS-VORMINGSBLADEN—monthly magazine.

STORM SS-weekly newspaper of the Dutch SS, subtitled at first BLAD DER NEDERLANDSCHE SS, and later changed to WEEKBLAD DER GERMAANSCHE SS IN NEDERLAND. First appeared on April 11th, 1941, and was published by Storm, Hekelveld 15A, Amsterdam-C. It continued to be published in Amsterdam until issue number 45 dated February 16th, 1945, but a second edition had appeared in Groningen starting with issue 26 dated September 29th, 1944. The Groningen issue ceased with number 5 dated May 4th, 1945.

VOOR VOLK EN VADERLAND—DE STRIJD DER NATIONAAL-SOCIALISTISCHE BEWEGING 14 DECEMBER 1931—MEI 1941, Nenasu, May 1941.

WAT IS WAT WIL DE GERMAANSCHE SS, Storm, Amsterdam.

WAT IS WAT WIL DE NEDERLANDSCHE SS, Storm, Amsterdam.

Sytze van der Zee, 25,000 LANDVERRADERS—DE SS IN NEDERLAND/ NEDERLAND IN DE SS, Kruseman, Den Haag, 1967.

(c) Belgium

GERMANISCHE REIHE, Flämische Ausgabe, Antwerpen—Flemish edition of the German SS monthly.

Edgar Erwin Knoebel, RACIAL ILLUSION AND MILITARY NECESSITY: A STUDY OF SS POLITICAL AND MANPOWER OBJECTIVES IN OCCUPIED BELGIUM, University of Colorado, 1965.

DE NATIONAALSOCIALIST—magazine.

PERIODIEK CONTACT—post-war monthly magazine for veterans of Belgian Waffen-SS and other units.

SS-KALENDER AAN ONZE FRONTKAMERADEN, "De SS Man", Antwerp.

SS-LIEDERENBOEK, Algemeene SS Vlaanderen—Flemish SS song book.

DE SS MAN—weekly newspaper of the Flemish SS, subtitled at first KAMPBLAD VOOR DE ALGEMEENE SCHUTSCHAREN-VLAAN-DEREN, but changed several times thereafter. First appeared on December 7th, 1940, and was published in Antwerp. Publication ceased with issue number 39 dated September 2nd, 1944.

DE VLAG, Uitgeverij "Steenlandt", Brussel—monthly magazine for the DeVlag movement. First issue appeared in late 1937, and the last was issue number 1 of the VIIth year of issue, dated August, 1944.

VLAMINGEN OP!—Flemish recruiting booklets for the Waffen-SS in various editions.

V.N.V.—KALENDER 1943.

VOLK EN STAAT—magazine of the V.N.V.

(d) Norway

EKSERSER-REGLEMENT FOR GERMANSKE SS NORGE, T.B.1, GJELDER FRA 1. JANUAR 1945, Oslo, 1945.

FRITT FOLK—daily newspaper of the Nasjonal Samling.

GERMANEREN—KAMPORGAN FOR GERMANSKE SS NORGE—weekly newspaper of the Norwegian SS. First appeared on July 25th, 1942, it was edited by SS-nestlagfører Egil Holst Torkildsen, and published by Hans S. Jacobsen. Publication ceased with issue number 17 dated May 5th, 1945, with the news of Hitler's death. The offices of "Germaneren" were at Akersgaten 8, Oslo.

GERMANISCHE REIHE, Norwegische Ausgabe, Oslo—Norwegian edition of the German SS monthly.

GERMANSKE SS NORGE MARSJERER, Oslo, 1944.

Asbjørn Hansen, GERMANSKE SS NORGE, Oslo, 1943.

Ralph Hewins, QUISLING—PROPHET WITHOUT HONOUR, The John Day Company, New York, 1966.

HIRDMANNEN—KAMPORGAN FOR RIKSHIRD OG NORGES SS—the official weekly paper of the Hird also served for the Norwegian SS before the introduction of "Germaneren" from issues dated May 24th, 1941, to April 4th, 1942, inclusive.

Franklin Knudsen, I WAS QUISLING'S SECRETARY, Britons Publishing Company, London, 1968.

MUNIN—DET NYE NORGE I BILDER—illustrated monthly magazine of the Nasjonal Samling, published by the Rikspropagandaledelsen. The first issue was for September 1942, and the last for April, 1945. An extra issue was produced called ALARM.

NORLANDIR—illustrated monthly magazine in German and Norwegian edited by Egil Holmboe. First issue appeared in December 1941, and the last in February 1945.

N. S. ÅRBOK 1942, Rikspropagandaledelsen, Blix Forlag, 1943.

N. S. ÅRBOK 1944, Rikspropagandaledelsen, Mariendals Boktrykkeri, Gjøvik, 1943.

"NY DAG" LOMME-ALMANAKK 1944, Rikspropagandaledelsen, Centralforlaget, Oslo.

SS-DAGEN 1943, Oslo, 1943.

(SS) GERMANSKE BUDSTIKKE—monthly magazine in Norwegian which started in 1941 with issue number 3.

(SS) GERMANSKE MÅNEDSHEFT—monthly magazine begun in 1941 but which continued for only the first two issues, then renamed (SS) GERMANSKE BUDSTIKKE.

SS-SANGBOK—Norwegian SS song book.

(e) Denmark

BESAETTELSESTIDENS FAKTA—DOKUMENTARISK HAANDBOG, J. H. Schultz Forlag, København, 1945—2 vols.

DAGGRY—TIDSSKRIFT FOR DET GERMANSKE FRONT— OG KAMPFÆLLESSKAB—monthly illustrated magazine started in 1944. It only ran to 11 issues and the last was number 8 of the second year of issue, dated April 15th, 1945.

D.N.S.A.P.s MAANEDSBREVE—monthly magazine of the D.N.S.A.P. which started in 1936 and ceased publication with issue number 11 of the 9th year of issue, dated February 1945.

FRIT DANMARKS HVIDBOK.

FÆDRELANDET—magazine.

GERMANISCHE REIHE, Dänische Ausgabe, Kopenhagen—Danish edition of the German SS monthly.

KAMPTEGNET

Vilh. LaCour, FRIKORPSET OG SCHALBURGKORPSET in: DANMARK UNDER BESAETTELSEN, Bind II, Westermann, København, 1946.

M. Lauritsen, I TYSK KRIGSTJENESTE in: DE FEM LANGE AAR—DANMARK UNDER BESAETTELSEN 1940-1945, Bind III, Gyldendahls, København, 1947.

K. B. Martinsen, FRIKORPS DANMARKS KAMPE, Copenhagen, 1944.

K. B. Martinsen, SCHALBURG KORPSET, Copenhagen, 194?.

NATIONAL SOCIALISTEN—KAMPBLAD FOR NATIONALSOCIALIS-MEN I DANMARK—weekly started in 1932 and which ceased publication with the issue dated May 4th, 1945.

(f) Switzerland

Jean-Baptiste Mauroux, DU BONHEUR D'ETRE SUISSE SOUS HITLER, J. J. Pauvert, Paris, 1968.

Walter Wolf, FASCHISMUS IN DER SCHWEIZ, Flamberg Verlag, Zurich, 1969.